The 9 Expressions of Love

How and Why We Choose Our Lovers

Carl E. Stevens, Jr.
Kenya K. Stevens

FIRST EDITION

ISBN: 978-1-7331648-2-5
Self-As-Source Publishing

Author: Carl E. Stevens, Jr. and Kenya K. Stevens
Published: September 2020

Web Address: https://www.progressiveloveacademy.com

CONTENTS

INTRODUCTION

We shouldn't question what we want in our lives...

What we want and desire is exactly what it *is*; what it *is* has merit and shouldn't be judged by us or others. There's wisdom in the organic, innate desire that is often overlooked in our society as superficial, carnal, or base—without depth. Our desires are seen as optional.

My wife, Kenya, and I married over 24 years ago. Our desires have shifted like the wind ever since. Even our desire for one another has changed over time. Sure, there were times when we both wanted our desires to be different; like everyone else in the West, we wanted to WANT one another, solely, like a normal monogamous couple. But we realized our desire for variety was overarching, and this was a challenge for us to navigate as an American couple. This is how we intuited the premise of this book.

By accepting our natural desires, even when they thwarted the Western monogamous model, we were able to feel into what we truly needed as humans outside of the parameters of society. This was an arduous process that we hope to make easier for you as you read this study.

Most of us have been taught to filter our desires based on what is socially acceptable. This is mostly due to the concept that desire, in and of itself, is negative. For instance, if we are in a marriage, it is held with disdain to desire another lover. This is based on social laws that prohibit or diminish any structure outside of monogamy. What would happen if this social construct was not yet known or not embraced by most? Would this same desire be shunned or deemed inappropriate?

We completely disagree with the premise that our desires are without in-depth meaning. Actually, we'd go as far as to say that the answer to our ills, problems, and life challenges can be solved by looking at what we desire. In other words, the solutions to our life challenges are *within* our desires. The mere fact that we have desires essentially implies we have everything we need to create the lives we desire.

Desire is how the *indwelling intelligence* within us leads to prosperity, peace, and happiness in our lives. Casting in our minds and hearts a sincere *want* that we then pursue leads us to joy, wholeness, and healing—what a blessing it is to have a simple way to know what we need at any particular time. Does this sound a bit too simple? Maybe it does, but the truth is we haven't been trained to utilize this innate key to living a successful and fulfilling life.

Our desires hold the key to our fulfilment as human beings; however, those desires must be adequately interpreted to deliver on such a promise of salvation. Let's look at an example to understand both the simplicity and underlying complexity before us. A simple one is our craving for a candy bar. Yes, the image of a chocolate-covered wafer appears in our minds. We see everything about the candy bar, from the store to buy it at to peeling back the wrapper and taking our first and final bite. It's so clear. The question, however, is whether the candy bar is the actual desire or if it simply represents the closest image our subconscious can relay to let us know we are perhaps glucose deficient at that very moment.

Maybe the image of the candy bar is being used to communicate the urgency of the glucose deficiency because our relationship with rice or vegetables wouldn't accurately relay the real need to our conditioned conscious mind. After all, we don't really relate vegetables to sugar or glucose. In addition, vegetables aren't a food source that most people crave or are addicted to. Therefore, the probability of prioritizing eating them is slim to none even when we are presented with a vision of them in our minds. Because most of us are addicted to sugar—the closest thing to glucose we can consciously relate to—our subconscious uses sugar-based food sources as a way to grab our attention and spark our interest. Who knows exactly how and why the subconscious mind communicates the way it does; regardless, wisdom is still found within the desire. An image of exactly what our body needs is sent straight from the operational control of our entire physiological system to our brain. We all know a picture is worth a thousand words. It doesn't get more efficient than that.

Pure desire is the most advanced communication mechanism known to man, woman, or child. But it's not only the image, right? It's also the ignition of our taste buds along with that image. We can literally taste that candy bar as if we are actually chewing it now. We get flashbacks of past experiences where we've eaten candy bars as well as a plethora of television commercials we've seen since childhood. Now, it's a full sensory experience—sight, taste, smell, touch, and the sound of the wrapper peeling back and us chewing. So good.

At this point, communication methodology from the subconscious to the conscious mind has become so powerful that most will have a hard time resisting its demands and drive straight to the closest store to buy that candy bar, right? We could actually call it *suggestion* rather than *communication* because of our inability to resist it in most cases. Most of us are familiar with the inherent truth within our desires. Even when we look at basics like hunger or thirst, those are desires that carry an inherent truth with them: we must drink water and eat food to survive, and the body needs both very soon. We never question that kind of desire, but we don't really think consciously about the truth that's being communicated either. We take it for granted. We know there's an innate truth and we trust it with our lives, but we don't really think about it in that context. We'd never forsake it, especially with our entire body reacting to the images being relayed to our brain. The stomach growling and our mouths watering. It's as real as it gets. It's a full-body experience that includes emotions and physical feelings. We don't deny it unless we've put ourselves on special dietary restrictions, in which case, we claim the desire isn't justified and should be ignored or transferred to an alternative need.

But let's be clear—wisdom is clearly relayed via the desire. However, the interpretation of the desire is where we get hung up. The need for glucose isn't best acknowledged with a candy bar. The need for vitamins, minerals, and protein isn't best fed with fast food. That's where we get things twisted and start questioning the wisdom inside of the desire instead of our interpretation of the image associated with the wisdom being communicated. In other words, we throw the baby out with the bathwater and essentially cut ourselves off from the one entity that knows exactly what we need, when, and how simply because we couldn't easily understand what it was trying to tell us.

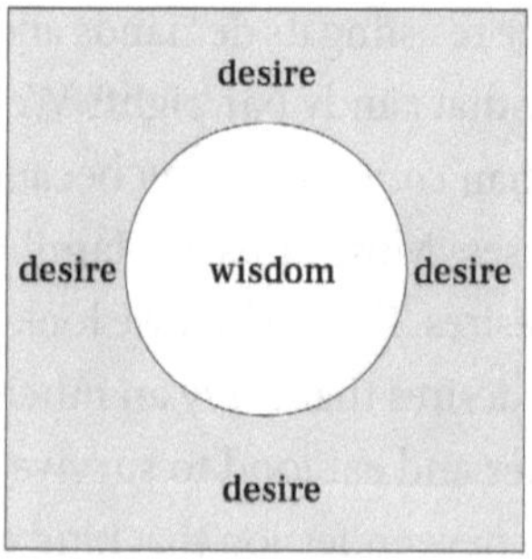

There's a saying: *all that glitters isn't gold*. It's also said that *everything is not what it may seem*. That's the difficulty with life—how can we receive the wisdom we need when we haven't been exposed to enough information or experience to clearly understand what we're attempting to interpret? We have an innate superintelligence within us that's literally simultaneously coordinating thousands of biological processes inside our bodies every second; when it needs more fuel or supplies, how can it communicate that to us? When it's low on vitamin K, B12, copper, or magnesium, what image should be used? What have you eaten in the past that contained the copper requirements that your body currently needs? Probably nothing. Ok, so what's the next closest thing? Who knows? It could be a doughnut or mint from a restaurant you ate at three years ago. So, we see the challenge. Our subconscious mind is attempting to talk to us about our needs, and when we misinterpret the image, we assume the wisdom is incorrect. "That must be my sugar addiction kicking in again. Let me ignore it completely and find something else to put my mind on," we might say to ourselves.

We used the food and hunger example because it's the easiest example to verify. When my body needs water, I get thirsty. Easy enough. How about when we need other things in our lives to maintain our health, needs, and sanity? Or when we need to maintain our mental health or our emotions? Is all we need as human beings food and water? Do we only need vitamins, minerals, proteins, carbohydrates, glucose, etc.? The answer is *of course not*. A study by researchers at **Washington University School of Medicine** in St. Louis found that children whose mothers nurtured them early in life have a larger hippocampus, a key brain structure that is essential to learning, memory, and response to stress according to a study published in the Proceedings of the **National Academy of Sciences Early Edition**. Another study found that when babies are not touched after birth, they die. They don't die from starvation, but rather from a lack of touch, intimacy, and human connection. Human beings are complex organisms. We need food and water, but we also need touch, love, connection, to be witnessed by others, and to witness others. We need sunlight, fresh air, space, and community. We need each other for survival. We need each other to maintain our sanity and a balanced state of mind. Typically, a harsh punishment for inmates in prison is solitary confinement, or being away from other human beings. Why? Because being away from other human beings (i.e., community) is a form of torture. What happens to most human beings when they're put into solitary confinement? They go insane. They lose their minds because they've lost an important part of their foundation and support—other humans.

Humans also need sex. The most powerful force within us is our creative or reproductive force. It's undeniable that we all have a powerful and unrelenting drive to procreate with other human beings. We all have a desire to bring our likeness into the world. The force is so strong that entire religions have been created to suppress it. From calling our desire and need to have sex a sin to punishing those who indulge in it, all cultures have attempted to curb our natural, human sexual desire. Rules, laws, and protocols have been created over centuries in an attempt to regulate our sexuality because it's just that powerful. The oldest trade on the planet is prostitution because the oldest and most profound need of human beings is sexual connection and expression.

As human beings, we are complex in our needs and expressions. The subconscious mind will always attempt to express to the conscious mind our most pressing needs as we move throughout our days and lives. This might include images of food, water, candy bars, and ice cream; images of people, places, and things; or images of love, sex, and connection—thus, the purpose of this book.

The 9 Expressions of Love™ attempts to bridge the conscious to subconscious mind communication gap that has become so prevalent in society today, especially regarding our relationship choices. One of the downfalls of human relationships is our inability to interpret the wisdom being communicated from our subconscious minds about who we should connect to, in what ways we should connect to them, why, and for how long. It's essentially our candy bar example playing out in relationships and sexuality. We think we need a candy bar when a steady dose of rice, fruits, and veggies over the next week is what we really need. We think we need to be in a long-term, committed relationship with person X when we really need intermittent intimacy from person Y. Or maybe we need to be with person X, but not in a committed relationship because what we need from them may not be something that's sustainable long term. Maybe person Y has the style of energy and companionship our bodies and psyches need to help us maintain our emotional health. Or maybe person Y has an electromagnetic charge that will help us rebalance our own energetic (i.e., emotional) imbalances, thus supporting us in staying off medications or sleeping better.

It's challenging to determine the primary reasons why our subconscious minds communicate to us about being connected to certain people at certain times, but we know there's wisdom there. As a culture whose relationship dissatisfaction has reached an all-time high, it is time to interpret that wisdom and attempt to apply it in the right way so we can benefit from it. If we want relationships to fulfill their intended purpose, it would be prudent to learn the language of the subconscious mind so we can start tapping into the wisdom that eighty percent of the brain scientists say we don't have access to—the subconscious mind. These conversations between our conscious and subconscious minds are very specific and personal, so it will be difficult for others to bridge that communication gap for us. We might be able to support with context clues and share our own interpretations, but in the end, we'll need to develop our own language and meaning.

If we do not begin to develop a science around interpreting relational desires, we will continue to judge ourselves and others for merely having yearnings that, for instance, can lead to adultery. In such a case, the subconscious is speaking to the conscious mind about a desire for someone other than our spouse. We receive the image as it becomes stronger by the day. Without an appropriate tool to analyze the desire we are feeling (i.e., the true need the subconscious mind is projecting onto the conscious mind), we feel compelled to follow that desire, which in turn could capsize our families and marriages. What if there was a way to interpret the desire and understand the true need the sub-mind is projecting to us? Could we achieve more fulfilling relationships, having analyzed our desires rather than following them blindly or attempting to ignore them altogether?

To begin this process of analyzing our desires, we must first acknowledge that communication is taking place from the subconscious mind (sub-mind) to the conscious mind. Next, we need to acknowledge that these sub-mind communications carry substantial weight in their ability to affect our choices. We discuss this in Part One of this book as we explore our natal desire to be dominant and to surrender in various relationship settings, as well as our natal aim to develop the feminine, masculine, and androgynous energies within us. We also explore a natural human need to escape from these boxes altogether. Detailed below are the key topics for the first part of this book:

- The position-roles of dominance versus submission versus neutrality in relationships
- The gender energies of masculine versus feminine versus androgynous expressions
- Combining positions and gender to give us nine total possibilities of expression

Then in Part Two, we'll move on to categorizing various types of relationship desires or expressions of love to make sense of who we should connect with and how.

The 9 Expressions of Love:

- Power Love
- Manifestation Love
- Freedom Love
- Supportive Love
- Soul Love
- Devoted Love
- Spiritual Love
- Romantic Love
- Physical Love

This can be so empowering because right now, we essentially have one relationship style that we feel good about—long-term, committed relationships within the context of marriage. All other relationship styles and formats are considered to be superficial, flighty, and sometimes irresponsible. They aren't looked at as something that should be regarded with any seriousness, and worse, they aren't considered an imperative need for our health and sanity as human beings; thus, many of us suffer as a result. We turn to opioids, alcohol, drugs, or destructive behavior as an alternative to the human connection we desire, which leads to addiction and self-destruction.

Clearly, we have deeper work to do on a societal level as well. We need to learn to trust ourselves so that we can trust one another. We need to believe one another when we say, "I love you" or when we desire a connection with someone. We need to honor what it means to be human beings so we can actually feel comfortable experiencing human emotions. We don't need to hold one another captive and expect everyone's expression of love to look the same or follow a rulebook.

Part Three rolls out the **Feminine Choice ParadigmTM**, which is about the authentic expression of our desire to connect with others as we feel led to do so. It's also about letting those people we've chosen know that our desire for connection is real, and it's safe for them to choose us back. Too often in our society, we don't believe that someone really, truly loves us and wants us in their life. Why? Maybe they aren't expressing that love in a way that we're familiar with or would like to see. Or maybe we'd like them to do for us what they did with their last partner. We can learn to accept love just as it comes. It's fine that it looks different from other relationships we may have seen or enjoyed. We'll create something brand new, special, and unique to us. It will be beautiful.

Choice goes both ways: *initial choosing* and then *choosing back*. But even before the process of being chosen comes an initial desire to be chosen in a very specific way; thus, a series of actions and positions takes place to potentially get us chosen in the way we'd like. This leads us to the **Masculine Desire Paradigm**™. Here, we discuss what it means for the masculine and dominant elements within us to (1) prepare themselves to be chosen, and (2) choose back when the feminine or submissive elements have made their choice. The

Masculine Desire Paradigm also helps us understand the source of our masculine and domination desires. This is the only way true connections can be made. We need to either fulfill the desires of our minds, spirits, and bodies or essentially choose back once we've been chosen if we are to have any hope of maximizing the gift of love and authentic connection.

Lastly, we talk about the **Illusion of Hypergamy**. Our culture is based on human-made laws, rules, and traditions, but the superintelligence within us operates beyond what we understand consciously. In other words, commitment must be redefined as something that represents authentic, unconditional love rather than something that is rules-based. This is critical; otherwise, we end up rejecting what we feel inside our hearts because those feelings go outside of established societal norms. Or worse yet, we may try to hide our true feelings and resort to sneaking around, which will ultimately make us sick, cause undue stress and anxiety, and destroy the integrity of our families and relationships.

Sneaking around can be misconstrued as a lack of love or respect instead of what it really is—**fear of allowing your truth to be seen by others who may judge or punish you for it.** We can't keep hiding the truth of who we are and how we feel, especially from our loved ones because they are the ones who are supposed to accept us regardless. It's an insane society where those we claim to love won't accept us for who we truly are and how we truly feel. **The 9 Expressions of Love** is about bringing sanity back to human connection and relationships. Let's free ourselves from undue burden and support ourselves and others in being free. Let's bring sanity back to love and our relationships.

Part 1: The Foundation

Understanding Dominance, Submission, & Neutrality

From a romantic standpoint, the discussion of one partner being in a dominant position and the other in a submissive position crushes the fantasy of the modern love story. Romantics might say, "Let's not get into the details of the *forces* that produce romantic feelings, forces that might denote *power dynamics* in relationships; instead, let's presume to be *equals* and walk into the sunset together, happily ever after." We totally get it and agree. It would be ideal to leave out the discussion around who is dominant and who is submissive when it comes to romance, but we'd warn romantics that pursuing the fantasy of romance also means accepting the tragedy of it. As much as humans have embraced the Western fantasy that love is about "equality," power dynamics such as dominance and submission are part of every relationship. In fact, constant interplay exists between many more forces than just these two and, in truth, it's the interplay of these forces that produces highs and lows and the flow and ebb that make romance so appealing.

We believe we romanticize equality because we want romance to be more predictable and more stable; equality is a concept that would seem to determine predictability as well as longevity. However, romance isn't about stability or longevity, is it? No. It's about feeling good in the moment and not worrying about tomorrow, but we all know that's not how serious relationships work. We know that *feeling good in every moment* is not how longevity in marriage is achieved. Marriage is a marathon, not a sprint, and takes planning, preparation, teamwork, discipline, commitment, communication, dominance, surrender, and wisdom—none of these sound romantic, but they are critical elements of successful long-term relationships.

The qualities that sustain long-term relationships are more complex than romance; they require full study into *power dynamics existing within the relationship.* For instance, teamwork requires knowing who will play which position and when—every team has positions. Weaving in the study of power dynamics, such as submission and domination, could mean an easy way to (1) describe who should lead and who should support the leader, and (2) note when that dynamic shifts. Without observations of strengths and weaknesses and acknowledgement of basic differences between individuals in relationships, it becomes impossible to create teamwork. And it's not only acknowledgement of differences; it's also the ability to embrace differences and allow them to become known dynamics.

For instance, a wife might be naturally dominant while a husband might be naturally more submissive, and this couple may go their entire marriage fighting this dynamic—simply because it's not romantic or even politically correct to acknowledge anything beyond *equality.* But when couples do not identify, define, or harness the natural dynamic, they cannot move beyond romance. And this is what all of us complain about: that we want more, we want depth and connection as well as commitment instead of fleeting "live in the moment/go with the flow" relationships. Yet how do we elicit teamwork, planning, cooperation, and the depth of communication it takes to move to long-term partnering without knowing about the various dynamics that are the foundation for how a potential team might work? We suppose we agree with romantics that the submissive versus dominant or power dynamics discussion should be avoided at all costs because this discussion was never intended for them.

For the rest of us who'd like our relationships to last forever, provide meaningful fulfillment, or even better, for those of us who want to understand who we're choosing as a life partner and why, observing the submissive versus dominant dynamic is critical.

Let's start with the foundational elements of this book, which utilize the combination of six components to establish why we've attracted and chosen our partner(s) and who we are inside of each relationship dynamic we manifest. These components are:

1. masculinity
2. femininity
3. androgyny
4. submission
5. dominance
6. neutrality

Before we get into the specific definitions for each component, let's understand what they represent collectively. These six elements describe *qualities of behavior* that we all exude and embody in some form throughout our lives.

The components of **masculinity, femininity, and androgyny** describe **how we tend to go about creating our lives.** They represent the **actual approach** and set of behaviors we utilize to get things done in the world. The components of **submission, dominance, and neutrality** describe the actual position **we assume when interacting with other people in relationships**, friendships, at work, with family, and in all areas of life. It's purely about where we place ourselves relative to other people before we even begin relating to them. It influences how we carry ourselves when moving about the world as a means of attracting a certain type of person into our lives. How we walk to how we dress and what car we drive can all be influenced by these components.

Submission, dominance, and neutrality are not goal-oriented outside of attracting specific types of people to connect with, but rather are relational in nature; in other words, they describe the role and position we play with another person inside of a relationship. Masculinity, femininity, and androgyny represent the approach or quality of energy we exhibit. So, we've taken the six components and broken them down into two categories:

a. **Masculinity, femininity, and androgyny** – our actual approach to effecting change in the world and our lives
b. **Submission, dominance, and neutrality** – the relative position we assume when interacting with other people

With these categorizations, we can move forward into specific definitions of each of the components.

Preponderance of the Submissive

There are two important components at play in the universe that are relevant to our discussions in this book: (1) energy, and (2) will. We'll discuss the role of **energy** when we cover the masculine and feminine interplay, but when it comes to submission versus dominance, we need to understand the **will**. It's our will that chooses our direction in life. Another explanation for our will is a combination of desire and choice. It's when we have a desire to have or do something and then choose the actions to realize that desire. Every action we take contains our personal desire and a subsequent choice to pursue that desire; in other words—our will.

When we describe submission, we are describing our relationship to our will. When you submit to someone, you're subjugating your will in deference to theirs. You make your desire to be in total alignment with their will and additionally choose to follow them at every turn. That's submission. It may sound like a powerless position, but whether we choose to interpret it that way or not, it's still a position we either accept or reject. Why would someone choose to submit their will to another? The short answer is the possibility of experience, learning, efficiency of effort, and growth. Perhaps others have processes that can move our lives forward and provide us with new skills or talents. Or maybe we have common goals that require a collective effort, but one person understands precisely how to get to where we're going. In that case, we'd gladly offer our energy and resources to them so that we can both achieve our goals.

Perhaps I need an experience in my life that will help me grow, but that experience isn't available except through a guide, teacher, or coach. In this case, I would need to **submit** my will to them to have that experience. We see this in the military where new recruits seek to understand what it means to be a soldier and submit their will to their commanding officers in order to learn. It's a complete dominance and submission relationship, and they'll even tell you not to think or do anything outside of what you're told to do. This is a perfect example of the will being subjected to the act of submission. New recruits are told, "Don't think. Do what you're told. Follow precise instructions." We find examples of submission in all areas of life, including work. If I'm learning to be an astronaut, it might serve me well to submit my will to those more experienced so I can learn to moonwalk, breathe, and effectively communicate with my team. Failure to submit my will during these training sessions can result in catastrophe depending on the job.

We can see from these examples that the prerequisite for submission should be submitting to someone with something substantial to offer us—from this perspective, it's a give and take relationship. The submissive person follows the dominant person and the dominant person gives the submissive person the experience they're looking for. That's the exchange. From the outside looking in, it may not appear to be an equitable arrangement, but upon closer examination, it becomes clear that both parties benefit.

With that said, we can clearly see situations where it's not beneficial to be submissive to another person. The most obvious example is where they either have nothing of value to exchange or lack the skills to properly transfer the desired experience the submissive person seeks. We have to realize that just because someone has an exceptional talent doesn't mean they understand how to transfer that knowledge. That's why it's said that geniuses in music make the worst teachers—although they are the most skilled and best performers, they lack the patience to work with others as well as an understanding of how exactly they obtained greatness.

But what about submission in relationships? Is there room for that kind of abandoning of the will? Of course there is. Successful relationships are all about the interplay of submissive and dominant roles being acted out by each partner; however, to fully comprehend how that works, we have to abandon the stereotype of what it means to be submissive in a relationship.

Being submissive is something that can take place by task, role, project, or in the relationship as a whole. Submission is not being a doormat or being abused by someone who doesn't care about you, love you, or have anything to offer. That's abuse, and subjecting yourself to that scenario means you're not in an empowered position and there is a lack of self-awareness. We're not talking about individuals who lack power or who don't realize their value.

You can't be in a submissive position without the realization of why you're there and without the ability to hold your partner accountable for holding up their end of the contract. Submission can get a bad name from people who don't actually choose it, but instead make a choice to subject themselves to abusive behavior as a way to punish themselves for not feeling worthy in life. Being abused has nothing to do with learning, growing, or achievement.

We each desire different things in relationships and our lives, and there are people out there who can provide those things to us while also obtaining what they desire from us. This is when submission works—when there is a mutual benefit between two parties.

It's important that we don't confuse submission with meekness or being weak. Submissive individuals can be very aggressive, especially when seeking a dominant person to submit to. They also carry a strength about them that actually allows them to serve others (i.e., dominants) in a substantial way. This can't be overstated enough. A five-degree black belt in martial arts is submissive to his or her teacher. A Navy Seal trained to kill is submissive to his or her commanding officer. So make sure not to confuse someone putting themselves in a submissive position with an indication of their capabilities around engaging the world around them.

Deference of the Dominant

The compliment to the act of submission is the act of domination. As previously stated, the person in the dominant position is someone with something to offer the submissive. They transfer that knowledge and experience by leading the submissive person through a series of guided experiences, which ultimately allows that knowledge to be transferred during the process. Or, they simply provide the value the submissive person is seeking as an exchange for being able to utilize their subjected will in whatever capacity they desire.

The value exchange between submissive and dominant characters can be material-based, an exchange for training, care, attention, labor, or otherwise. We should be careful not to judge what people find as an exchange in these scenarios. We should also be careful not to give into popular stereotypes about who actually has the upper hand in the dominance versus submission relationship dynamic. Submission and dominance form a circular relationship structure, not a hierarchical one. These are both roles that each person chooses to play, even when it appears no alternative choices are available. That being said, it's true some people will try to force dominance over others in certain situations, but even then, the submissive must agree, because an important element to being a dominant person is having the respect of those who've submitted to you. The respect element is what separates a true dominant from a dictator.

When someone is in the dominant position, it means they are the head. They dictate the movements of everyone involved and steer things toward the desired outcome. Dominance is incorrectly viewed as a position of strength because it's assumed the person forced their way into the dominant position against the will of the submissive person. Or, they assumed that position because others saw them as stronger and simply submitted to their will. Another way to state it is that people give others power out of fear or insecurity. Actually, that's not a form of dominance, but rather the respect of another's power. It falls under the domain of someone's response to feminine or masculine energetic expression. It's when someone utilizes a tactic (e.g., force, coercion, power, threats, etc.) to achieve an end and others respond in kind. For example, if I get into a fight with someone and they physically overpower me, my options are to surrender—which means, I'll stop my attack and back off—or to fight until the end (i.e., death).

My decision to yield isn't submission, but rather an agreement to stop using force at that moment. How about if a police officer tells me to move off of someone's property and I do it? Did I submit? Maybe in a way, but that's actually compliance. I didn't submit my will to the police officer but instead complied with their command in order to avert potential harm to myself. Compliance means I'm reluctantly doing what's being asked or ordered of me. I was on the property because I wanted to be there and if the police officer didn't ask me to move, I wouldn't have moved. In addition, our original definition of submission requires us to gain something in return for submitting. In this case, fear of loss isn't in the spirit of the definition. In other words, we don't submit for our safety, but rather because we gain something that we want by doing so. There's a difference. When we know there are no speed traps on the highway, most of us choose to drive without regarding the speed limit. It doesn't mean we'll speed necessarily, but we won't prioritize the speed limit above our will and desires. That's why following an order from an authority figure is considered compliance and not submission, as it's not something we would normally desire to do outside of avoiding punishment or personal harm. When we sign up for the military, we know what it's all about. We know we'll be taking orders for our entire service tenure; therefore, our desire to submit is a prerequisite for joining the military. We submit our will to the military before we even submit our application. What about if a dictator takes over the country and forces people to follow their rulership? This is also compliance since we'd rather not do it. As a matter of fact, the only reason we're doing it is to save ourselves from death or pain. Is that dictator in the dominant position? Stereotypically, yes, but technically, no. They possess the greatest amount of force and their position represents the reality that no one else in the country has an equal amount of force at their disposal. Ruling by fear doesn't make one a dominant person. One must have the respect of those who comply with their dictates. In short, if you hand your followers all of the guns and power but they choose to give it back to you out of respect, you're dominant.

Staying with the theme of fear, we can't really learn anything when we are in a constant state of anxiety and tension, and a true dominant knows this. A truly dominant teacher knows how to raise and lower the levels of anxiety their students might be experiencing because that's how the natural growth process takes place. Growth is a combination of rest and tension that supports the student in becoming receptive to an experience. Incidentally, this is why many children don't realize their potential in school because the teacher isn't in a mindfully dominant position. Yes, the teacher may be in charge and can steer the children's behavior in the way they desire, but that doesn't translate into the children learning the lessons. Why? Because to be dominant, we must have the respect of those in our care. When that happens, they become submissive to us—or in this case, to the lessons we are attempting to teach them—and can take it in (i.e., learn). Ideally, a teacher wants a student to submit their will (i.e., all the things they don't know about calculus) so they can take in everything the teacher knows about a subject. This is the only real way knowledge transfer can work.

The only way to truly gain from what the dominant has to offer is through submission. In other words, there's no other way for one to organically grow in the experience than through submission, because certain experiences must be real in order to work. They need to evoke genuine emotion without allowing us to exercise the right to drop out when the going gets rough. If I know the haunted house is fake, I'm not really going to be scared in the same way as when I don't know this information. Life is the best teacher, and the best way to learn life's lessons and spurn growth is to mimic it. Thus, the person in the dominant position must have complete control to hold up their end of the bargain. What the submissive person is offering is something that doesn't require control or dominance. They aren't offering lessons per se, but rather (1) a strengthening in what the dominant person is already delivering, and (2) an energetic or material offering that could essentially be obtained anywhere but at a different exchange rate (i.e., money, etc.). An example of this is a martial arts guru giving their student the sacred teachings of Kung Fu in exchange for cleaning and tending to their house. What the guru has can't be found anywhere, but what the student gives in exchange is easily replicable by others in the community. This is a necessary component of the exchange; otherwise, the submissive could easily become the dominant simply based on the concept of supply and demand. For example, if that same student is paying the rent and utilities for the guru's dojo, it may affect how hard the guru pushes the student because of their need for them not to walk away, therefore bankrupting the company. The dominant must be firm in their position and autonomous relative to the actions and behavior of the submissive in order to deliver their offering. If the submissive doesn't deliver on their promise, it simply means they don't get the experience of being educated by the dominant.

It should be clarified that the dominance versus submission

dynamic is applicable only when one or both people have a quality that is an attraction point—a quality that draws people to them. Sometimes people get confused and think that because they have a certain skill or do a certain amount of work, it means they are in a dominant position in a relationship. This is simply not true. Just because one person makes all the money in the relationship, handles all the bills, does the taxes, etc., this doesn't put them in the dominant position. Their partner must see those financial qualities as an attraction point for it to bring in the dominance versus submission dynamic. Without this attraction point, it's simply a set of skills and responsibilities that one partner has that supports the maintenance of the relationship.

What brings human beings together is attraction and sexual desire. Regardless of what we want to tell ourselves, that's still the foundation of why we are drawn to one another. It doesn't mean we don't choose partners based on other criteria because we certainly do; however, those criteria don't alter the fundamental truth of what drives us to mate as human beings. All we're saying here is that these attractions are founded in a number of different areas, and the person with the strongest attraction point tends to be the submissive in the relationship.

Seclusion of the Neutral

Implicit in dominance or submission is the propensity and desire to connect with others. It's a need, actually. The dominant person isn't complete without a submissive person to guide. What's the use of gaining mastery if we can't share our lessons with others? The submissive person is lost without a dominant person's guidance because our gateway to understanding is exponentially streamlined when working with a master of the art. The person who's neutral, however, is the soloist. They have no desire to be completed by another or to connect with anyone. That's what separates them from everyone else. Neutral people tend to be the doers in society and prefer the application of what they know toward specific ends. Even in the absence of knowledge and understanding, the neutral person would rather press forward and learn from the experience itself instead of taking the shortcut of learning through a master. This is also a noble path to follow because of the rewards of the journey, even though the amount of time, energy, and effort expended could potentially be something we'd come to regret. From another perspective, those that adopt a neutral stance in life could also be the recluses or those who just want to be left alone to live their lives on their terms. They're not out to prove anything and may have already had the submission or domination experience.

Additionally, the neutral person may have the ability to be dominant and may understand that submission is our greatest teacher and is something we should always be open to, but have no preference as to which role they play. This dynamic exists outside of dominance versus submission and the idea of just being with self, and is instead focused on playing any role required for success in life. The neutrality position-role is important because it gives us context for how to be either dominant or submissive. It also allows us to go deeper into ourselves and have an appreciation for why we might want to explore a particular position-role. In addition, it can offer us a chance to rest, take a break, and find peace within.

It's also important in that this dynamic marks a level of independence—an inner contentment allowing us to be free of the need to interact with others even though the willingness is there. At some point, we must be ready to apply what we've learned without having to involve others. We must graduate from needing guidance (i.e., submissive role) or from sharpening our skills by guiding others (i.e., dominant role) to just being within our existing skill set and confidence level. This is what it truly means to be neutral.

It should be noted that the lack of desire or need to connect with others is also an attractive force in many ways. It's often those who lack this need that become the most appealing.

Dominance, Submission, & Neutrality in Relationships

We've covered the technical details of dominance and submission as states of being, but how do they apply to relationships? Is one person dominant over another in a marriage? Remember, this relationship is circular; there's no hierarchy here. There's no top and bottom, but instead, there are roles we each play inside the relationship to make it work. Are these like traditional gender roles? No, because traditional gender roles are based on cultural dynamics, whereas dominance and submission are based on (1) our individual preferences toward behavior and function, and (2) what we may be looking for in a relationship. Traditional gender roles tend to ignore personal preferences and instead predefine our behavior in marriage regardless of our personal desires or skills. Does this mean traditional gender roles are bad? No, it doesn't. They work perfectly for some people, but at the end of the day, it needs to be a choice.

There are two ways to look at how submission and dominance play out in relationships: (1) multiple roles are required to make a relationship work and each partner will play one or the other based on the task or area of responsibility, or (2) the primary way each partner desires to love and be loved inside the relationship is a condition for them being a part of the relationship in the first place. In the latter, we're making the assumption that each partner has a definite preference for how they'd like to be loved over the course of the relationship that fits their needs, desires, and personality. Usually, this is of such importance that it's considered a make-or-break condition for any relationship they enter into. We'll discuss the nine primary categories that capture all possible preferences we may have later in the book. For example, for some people, it may be important to be looked at as the unequivocal leader of the family and relationship by those observing from the outside (i.e., family and friends) because it makes them feel loved and respected, which is a prerequisite for them being able to love. For others, it's simply loyalty and specialness. As long as their wants, needs, and desires are their partner's top priority, they'll feel fulfilled in the relationship. Still for others, it's the ability to express their freedom and not be boxed into the monotony of any one relationship style. It really depends on the person, but let's not make any assumptions based on these examples. Let's not assume that the person who wants to be seen as the unequivocal leader of the family is dominant because it's not that straightforward, as we'll come to see later.

In many cases, we're attracted to someone because they look so beautiful or handsome. We're just captivated by their looks. This is an example of us putting ourselves in a submissive position in the relationship. The gorgeous person is in the dominant position and we are attracted to them and desire to be with them because of their beauty. Maybe they represent the fantasy of what we always thought beauty would be and we really want to be associated with it. The very fact that we want to be with someone because of their beauty means that we see them as having something that we desire for ourselves. How do we know this? Because if we weren't captivated by their beauty, there wouldn't be a strong draw to be with them. We might appreciate their beauty, but we'd not be drawn to be with them because of it. We see this often in relationships where we meet someone who looks good but would need to present something else in order for us to be interested in them like that. Maybe we need to see what their personality is like first before we open up to them and get to know them better. But we've all been captivated by beauty before and we know what that looks like, right? Their personality and character are a second-hand consideration and not necessarily a deal-breaker in order to be with them. In this circumstance, why would the handsome person agree to be with you if they, in fact, see themselves as superior in the looks department? It's just like we described earlier where the dominant sees value in the submissive if the latter is willing to supply what the former needs from them. Maybe the dominant desires financial support from the submissive, or maybe they need help with a business venture. This is the mutual exchange that's taking place. However, mutual is not necessarily the same as equal, especially as the submissive is literally captivated by the beauty of the dominant. Therefore, they are more desirous of the relationship to move forward. Maybe they know that the number of handsome individuals willing to give them an opportunity is limited; thus, their willingness to do what's required is greater. However, the dominant knows they really don't need much financial help right now and could hire someone to help them with their business in the future. Thus, the dominant and submissive relationship dynamic is established.

Maybe someone has an attraction to a person because of their financial wealth. They have nice cars, a home, credit cards, and the freedom and ability to take trips whenever they desire. If the submissive is desirous of that lifestyle or being around those types of individuals, they would be willing to submit their will to the dominant. The dominant person will expect certain favors and compliance in return. Is it always about simply living a rich lifestyle? Of course not. Oftentimes, we're just looking to be in that energy or to improve our own financial acumen and know the value of being associated with those who've accumulated wealth. Maybe this particular relationship is just for a season and once the submissive develops a wealth mindset, they'll be ready to move on to another relationship dynamic that will teach them the next lesson they desire to learn. The wealthy person is the dominant, and the person seeking wealth is the submissive.

Is the wealthy person always the dominant? No. For example, some people accumulate wealth for the sake of having access to beauty. We all know individuals who buy expensive cars in order to impress their friends and potential partners. In these cases, the wealthy person is the submissive and the beautiful person they are pursuing is the dominant. See how it works? The same thing goes for the handsome person or the guy who works out every day in the gym to get his body right. He's not always the dominant, especially when his motivation for a perfect body is to obtain love, affection, or money. Maybe he shaped his body that way to have women of means pay him for his time, thus pulling him out of the work world. Maybe he desires to be associated with other beautiful people and worked his way into getting chosen by the women of his dreams. In that case, he could be in the masculine-submissive position while the women choosing him are the feminine-dominant. We'd have to look deeper to be sure, but the point is that everything isn't always as it seems in the realm of dominance, submission, and neutrality.

It's hard to really judge from the outside when trying to determine who is submissive versus dominant. Only *we* really know why we've chosen to be with a particular person and that's what this book is for—to offer us clarity on why we choose someone in a relationship so that we can function accordingly to support the relationship in being successful.

These examples give us an overall blueprint for the relationship and tell us who takes on the role of primary submissive and primary dominant. This is important because if these basic criteria aren't met, we can see problems arising in the marriage; if they are met and honored, we find an overall successful marriage. Does this mean one person is submissive and one person is dominant for every aspect of the relationship? No, not necessarily. There can be other areas where the submissive is actually dominant. Let's say that the wealthy man is the submissive and the beautiful woman is the dominant. He's submissive because his primary driver for being financially successful is to have access to a beautiful woman and one day have a beautiful wife. The wife is the dominant because she is confident in her beauty and feels she can attract a number of men, including those with money. She is simply looking for a great partnership that is loving and supportive, and will look at a variety of options when selecting a mate. The man, however, is looking for a wife who is beautiful in his eyes and the eyes of society. As a result, she's the dominant. Let's say they are married and have children and he proves to be an amazing father and husband. He is present with her and very attentive to their children. He realizes that love and respect for his skills as a father makes her feel that she has a special man as a husband, which puts him in a special place in her heart. This is not just about the fact that he is the children's biological father, but also that he's demonstrated supreme gifts in that area. In addition, she gets to see her shortcomings as a parent and mother through observing his dedication; thus, she becomes submissive to him and he becomes dominant within the auspices of child-rearing. She recognizes that she has much to learn in this area and appreciates what he brings to the table as a parent while simultaneously wanting to be better herself. Parental excellence wasn't a criterion for her to be with her husband, but it became important after having children.

NOTE: She's still the primary dominant in the relationship because the First Choice™ determines the foundation of the union and also becomes non-negotiable in the relationship contract. We can say her being a submissive because of his parenting skills is a secondary choice. Following this same example, as they enter their later years, the husband begins to appreciate his wife in terms of how she takes care of him. Her consistency in feeding, nurturing, and caring for him when he's sick is something he's grown an appreciation for over the years. It's something that has helped him go beyond an appreciation for her beauty to an appreciation for her dedication to his well-being. For this reason, he sees her as irreplaceable in his life, thus making her the dominant once again in the relationship. Now, she holds a primary and secondary dominant position as well as a secondary submissive position, while he holds a primary and secondary submissive position (because of her nurturing) as well as a secondary dominant position. These positions don't have to necessarily be communicated, but doing so helps us recognize them when they come up. In other words, when we recognize a profound love or appreciation for our partner, it is best to honor this recognition in the relationship.

There are other areas in relationships involving responsibility that aren't the same as dominance. Just because someone has expertise or responsibility in an area, they are not automatically dominant in the relationship or in that area. Remember, dominance and submission involve the concept of choice and why one person would choose to be with another. One partner could be amazing and sexually skilled, but if the other partner doesn't see that as a reason to be with them, the dominance and submission dynamic wouldn't apply. In another example, the wife is in the primary responsibility position within the family when it comes to the children because she has taken on most of the responsibility for their care and upbringing. Perhaps the amount of time she spends with the children far exceeds that of the husband, which makes her the authority on what the children need, their primary desires, and any special considerations critical for their development. As a result, the husband defers to her authority in the area of child-rearing. However, if the husband doesn't see her motherly abilities as an attraction point for being with her, she would not be the dominant in that area.

How Monogamy Reinforces Feminine Submission

It's important to be aware of where we get our perspectives from on the masculine and feminine as unequal expressions of energy. The same goes for the perception that submission is weakness and dominance is strength. These ideals are cultural, but they are reinforced with our relationship styles—mainly monogamy. Because we believe the masculine is superior and dominant, where does that leave the feminine? It leaves it and women in the subordinate position relative to men. Thus, the monogamous relationship structure is a box that reinforces these cultural beliefs. Does that mean monogamy is bad? No, but it does mean the modern, cultural definition of monogamy is extremely harmful because it reinforces the subordination of women. If we are monogamous—which we aren't—a woman's role relative to a man is a subordinate. In other words, she's automatically deemed as someone who is lesser than. This is a big deal because there's no more important cultural institution than that of family and marriage. Not only is the lesser message being propagated, but also remember the submissive is learning from the dominant in exchange for a non-specialized contribution. This means men, by cultural association, primarily have the valuable life skills, wisdom, and offerings. Again, the implication is that women are the lesser.

Monogamy won't allow the man to be the feminine (i.e., submissive) because that's just not how marriage is structured. Men wear the pants—they are dominant and masculine—while women honor and follow their husbands. We know it sounds kind of old school, but these beliefs are firmly ingrained in our DNA. This is why we see women as the primary pursuers of marriage in our culture, because in order to be valuable, they must be validated (i.e., chosen) by men in marriage. He must find you worthy of transferring what he has to offer. If a woman isn't chosen by a man in marriage, her value is immediately assessed as lower than the standard. What's wrong with her? Maybe she has issues. Basically, the longer she goes unmarried, the lower her value gets. These are the cultural and dating realities many women battle against in our society, and they're very real. Again, in monogamous culture, the man is masculine and dominant, while the woman is feminine and submissive. In a monogamous culture, submissive means subordinate and feminine means weakness, whereas dominant means authority and masculinity means strength. In modern monogamous culture, it's believed that human beings are naturally monogamous. Thus, the established order of men and women is written by God and nature and therefore stands as truth. We can see the challenge with this thinking, but it doesn't stop there. Of course, man being the superior, dominant being means he isn't equal to women; thus, dating multiple women (infidelity or otherwise) is perfectly justified.

If he's not equal, he surely can't be with just one woman, and having affairs is the natural order of things. Could this be why men have felt more justified in practicing infidelity over centuries, because, well, it's expected? To move further, why would single women participate in the infidelity of married men? Maybe it's the natural competitive environment that's been created by those whose self-worth has reduced them to second-class citizens. Desperation calls for extreme measures, right? Or maybe being chosen in any capacity by a man is a form of validation of one's worth. Thus, infidelity is a part of a monogamous culture where women exist on the following tiers: (1) level one – wifey material, (2) level two – courtesan, and (3) level three – the unchosen and unworthy. From this perspective, we can see how women would accept level two over level three, just like we can see men doing their natural duty and supporting women in finding their proper placement in the world by having affairs.

It's important to have these conversations so we know how we got here in our current dating cultural scenario. Given that men can seemingly be so selective when it comes to marriage due to their perceived greater value inside of the institution, we can see why men hold women to standards of things like a low "body count" and vanilla sexual history, rather than accepting them for who they are. Maybe men have a lower tolerance for their wives cheating because it ruins the fantasy of her being wifey material; instead, she is a courtesan as defined by another man. Now that's a shot to the ego! The woman you assessed as a wife is later reassessed as a courtesan by the brotherhood. So then what does that say about you as a man having chosen a level two woman as a wife? You must be less than a man and someone on the level of a woman, god forbid. This could be why a low body count is so important as a prerequisite for a woman, as it reduces the number of men that can categorize her as a level-two woman. Naturally, the more men she's been with, the higher the probability of her being categorized as a courtesan or as unchosen and unworthy by those men, and if word gets out, it could damage the man's brand. What a tangled web we weave in monogamous culture. This might explain why monogamous marriage has such a high failure rate—women know they aren't actually subordinate and that most men aren't actually dominant. Maybe the magic that's supposed to happen after we say, "I do" never happens, and all that's left is each other in our rawest form, standing there left to work it out. Here's where we see that having a chip on your shoulder—where one shouldn't exist—can be a serious problem. What happens when men can't deliver on that dominant thing? When is the legend bigger than the man? Drama. Divorce. Alimony. Feminism.

This is why a metaphysical approach to masculine and feminine energy, as well as submissive versus dominant postures in relationships, is so needed. We must re-educate ourselves on who we actually are and what our potential contributions to our relationships can be, but we can't do that if we believe that we're something we're not. We can't do that if we don't even know what our potential is because we're trapped in a box of lies and labels. We guess it's time for us to move forward with a level head about ourselves and create a reality that reflects what we actually desire and not what society expects of us.

The Importance of Masculinity, Femininity, & Androgyny

There's so much talk about what it means to be masculine or feminine that we're on information overload. The challenge is the information that's available lacks a solid foundation to support its assertions. The first thing we need to understand is what the masculine and feminine actually represent—they are descriptions and categorizations of people's behavior. We use these designations to better understand who we are as individuals and as a collective society. What we know is that there are ranges of responses to life situations, and although each situation is specific unto itself, general categorizations can help us understand the best ways to respond. For example, if you're about to be attacked by someone with a weapon, we can generalize that a masculine response would generally be beneficial in increasing your chances of survival. Conversely, if you are being bullied in school, it may be best to utilize a feminine response to the bully for the sake of your safety and the greater good of the community. Sure, you could attack the bully, but because your life isn't in danger, it's not a necessity or the most intelligent way to handle the situation.

The second thing to understand is that the masculine and feminine designations are not synonymous with gender in the absolute sense. This means the word reference of "masculine" doesn't equate to male and the word reference of "feminine" doesn't equate to female, just like "female" doesn't equate to a woman and "male" doesn't equate to a man. Female and male are biological and scientific descriptions given to human beings with certain physical traits regardless of their age or behavior. Because we're untying the masculine and feminine from gender designations, we must also disconnect them from gender roles. This is because gender roles are cultural, while masculine and feminine energetic designations are metaphysical. It's simply two different systems of evaluating human behavior which can't be adequately compared. It's almost like measuring the volume of fluids in a jar using a measurement of inches. It just doesn't work.

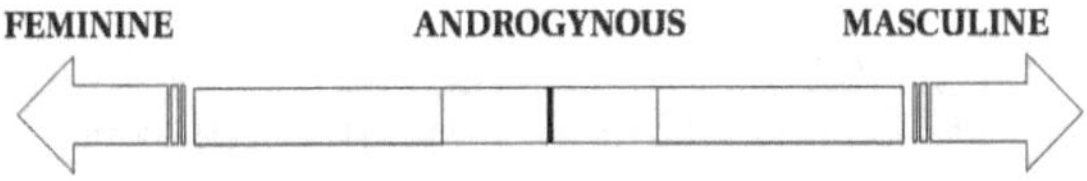

Lastly, masculine, feminine, and androgynous gender designations hope to capture a wide spectrum of human behavior, but because we all evaluate human possibilities differently, it must be noted that these designations are subjective and only make sense relative to their complementary behavior. *Nothing in the world can be evaluated by itself, but only relative to something else.* This isn't just true for the material in this book, but for everything in life. Therefore, it's a waste of time to debate about specific behavior designations as being masculine, feminine, or androgynous without also identifying their compliment.

So, in our exercise of looking at masculine, feminine, and androgynous expressions, we're essentially identifying complementary expressions of behavior. Our philosophy is similar to that of the Taoist philosophy that denotes yin and yang energetic expressions as compliments to one another. They don't exist without each other. We're saying that the feminine is the compliment to the masculine and vice versa. We're also saying that androgynous is complementary to itself. In addition, the feminine can be complementary to an androgynous element if need be, particularly in the absence of a masculine element. If we were to take away all of the masculine elements in the universe, the androgynous elements automatically become the best compliment to the feminine and vice versa. Again, the law that rules qualitative analysis is the law of relativity, as nothing has a quality in and of itself.

Lastly, we're simply describing behavior without judgment or the need to insert morality or philosophical beliefs because that's an entirely different exercise. This discussion isn't about what's right or wrong, but rather how energy moves and the best way to classify these behaviors relative to each other. Why? Because right and wrong are relative designations and completely subjective. With that said, let's delve a bit deeper.

The Feminine Illustrated

We often hear both the feminine and masculine described as energy, which is accurate when understood in the proper context. Energy is something we will go into greater detail later in the book, but for now, it's best defined as a motivating force that moves us based on its particular quality at any time. So, it's true there are a group of energies that move us toward being masculine and another group of energies that move us toward being feminine.

Feminine expressions and approaches to accomplishing tasks and goals in life are defined as anything that utilizes power as its primary means of achievement. Power is accumulated when energy is channeled inward and subsequently stored and circulated to be potentially utilized at a later time or for a specific purpose. The result of energy being stored is that it causes the object using it to be still and stand firm in its current position. Feminine energy means standing firm in one's current position regardless of the push or pull of outside influences. Feminine energy is also expressed by following established paths and maintaining current cycles in order to reduce effort and accumulate power via momentum. This contradicts the narrative that feminine energy is about going with the flow (which is actually a state of androgyny). Although feminine expression follows established paths, it will not change directions to follow a less resistant or more efficient path, just like it won't attempt to challenge a more difficult path.

This apparently contradicts the idea about the feminine going with the flow at the behest of the masculine. The feminine element has a reputation for following the masculine and allowing itself to be led by it. But this isn't totally accurate. The masculine gender energy actually leads other masculine elements, whereas the feminine attaches itself to the masculine, which can appear as following even though it's not actually doing so. The feminine stands firm in its position with the masculine and thus goes with it wherever it goes. This isn't following; rather, it is bonding.

In addition to this energy being used at a later time, the process of continually storing it causes energy to accumulate, thus increasing exponentially over time. This means it builds upon itself and becomes more effective as a tool for achieving in the world. An example of gathering energy is charging a mobile phone battery while the phone is turned off. You could say the power of the battery increases the longer the phone is on the charger. You could also say the battery gathers power faster when the phone is not being used compared to when it's in use. Once the battery is charged to maximum capacity, the phone can be removed from the charger and stored for potential use. Once the phone is in use, it begins to lose power. In other words, its power dissipates and its potential to get future work done decreases. *The process of utilizing energy to increase one's power and potential is feminine expression.* So, how does this work? The fully charged phone has a certain effect on people and the environment. As an owner, your behavior, including your confidence, is altered knowing you have a phone with a full battery. You know that when you need to use it, it will be there. You're confident about that. That confidence and surety with the ability to back it up when needed is power and feminine expression. If you're on a long road trip with your family and everyone is on their phone except you, you'll see your power on display the longer the trip, especially if charging options are limited. But what happens when everyone in the car knows you have a fully charged phone that you haven't even turned on yet? They begin to look to you for future support—maybe to make a call, to check their social media, to see what the weather is going to be, or for use in an emergency. If the car dies and everyone's phone is low on battery charge, it puts you in the power position. You can be on the phone for hours from that point if need be. Is this important? It can be if it's night-time and someone needs to walk to the gas station five miles down the road, and you have the only available flashlight option on your phone. Moreover, you have the only GPS option that will work for the duration of you getting to your emergency destination. If everyone's phone is dead but yours is fully charged, you become a powerful person in that emergency scenario. Does it mean other people in the car have no value? No, it doesn't, but they dissipated all of their energy so there is no more potential—they only have memories of playing games for the first four hours of the trip.

Another practical example is with money. We all know that people who have a lot of money are considered to be powerful people in society. They often don't even need to spend their money because people know they have it. They get the best tables in restaurants, the kindest and most respectful treatment, the greatest discounts available, and are approached by the most desirable people. We've always said that the more money you have, the less you have to spend on many of the same goods and services available to everyone. How did these individuals gain power? They channeled energy inward. In this case, money is an energy indicator. Did they spend all the money that came to them? No. They stored it. They kept it in their bank and investment accounts, which increased the potential of that money. The greater the potential to influence the world, the more respect the world gives it; thus, these individuals become powerful people. They are powerful because they are the executors of the stored energy reserves or, in this case, the liquid cash and assets. They are also powerful because of their demonstrated ability to store and reserve energy and things of value where the average person isn't able to do it. The average person spends the money they earn and continues to live paycheck to paycheck without leveling up financially. In other words, it takes a certain quality to be able to harness energy and store it for later use. It also takes a certain quality of character (i.e., power) to not indulge in temporary and superficial pleasantries for the sake of a more substantial future. It's the stored money that is the representation of a person's power. When that executor dies, the new executor assumes control of those assets and the power that comes with them. However, if the new executor doesn't have the same quality of character as the previous executor, we can expect those assets to dissipate. This is why we see children spending their inheritance quickly. They sell houses and liquidate assets and are soon left with nothing. Why do they do that? Because they don't have the inherent quality of being powerful people, which is a specific feminine expression.

The previous two examples dealt with external objects that serve as a representation of the owner's power, but they apply to us physically and mentally as well. If a fifth-degree black-belt, world champion heavyweight boxer, or Navy Seal walks into a room, their power will be felt immediately. Everyone in the room knows their potential and acts accordingly. How did they gain that power? They trained, practiced, lifted weights, studied, competed, and took that additional muscle mass, muscle memory, and fighting skill and stored it for future use. They don't have to actually use it (i.e., force) to gain respect or favor from the people around them. It's given automatically because they have power. Everyone knows their potential to seriously hurt or kill another human being; thus, respect is given. The same works with the mental. When Albert Einstein walked into a conference room, respect was given without him having to say a word. Why? Because he was powerful. He stored energy in the form of rigorous study, reading, experimenting, writing, defending theories, presentations, debates, gathering information, and learning through experience. His potential was great because he didn't waste his mental capacity on drugs, alcohol, or activities that wouldn't elevate him. He's not the only genius in the world, but he's one of the ones who maximized and grew his potential—and for that, he's gained tremendous respect.

Another way to express power—and thus, their feminine expression—is in one's ability to magnetize or attract what they desire. In the previous examples, you could say the boxer, Navy Seal, and fifth-degree black-belt attracted respect. Essentially, they pulled the action of respect out of others and bestowed it upon themselves. For most people, internalizing their energy for the sake of attracting others is intentional. In other words, many of us desire the attention and respect we get from others. This can be said about many celebrities who have dreamed of being cheered on by huge crowds of people. You could say they engaged in particular activities that increased their power and thus attracted mass appeal and attention from others, which of course attracted financial prosperity as well. When a young woman spends countless hours shopping for clothes; learning to do her make-up; getting facials, her nails, hair, and lashes done, teeth whitening; and practicing her posture and how to present herself in a soft way, she's doing so to increase her attractiveness. She's making herself more powerful; thus, she will be more attractive and will expect to draw men to her. Not only will she expect to draw men to her, but also favor, attention, and deference from others. This is femininity at its finest. This is what women mean when they say they want to be more attractive to the opposite sex. They want the ability to draw men to them without having to approach them or say or do anything in particular. They want to be aggressively yet respectfully pursued by potential partners. They want offers of kindness, free drinks, food, gifts, compliments, and the like. The more power she gathers, the greater the attraction quantitatively, but also the higher quality of a man she attracts. This is the meaning behind the saying, "beauty is pain," because of the time and energy required to increase one's power and attractiveness. Men often engage in the same behavior. When a man spends an excessive amount of time in the gym lifting weights, one of his goals is to sculpt his body such that his power is increased and he can easily attract women. When women see him walking along the beach with his shirt off, he's essentially drawing them to him. This is a power play. The same can be said for men who focus on their clothing and wardrobe and always dress exceptionally well. It's the same power play, just in a different area. They are hoping to attract attention from women who identify their handsome attire as an elevated status of their intelligence, as well as their financial and reproduction potential. Are we saying that weightlifting or consistently wearing nice clothes is a feminine trait? No, not in and of itself. However, lifting weights and sculpting your body for the purpose of attracting attention is without a doubt feminine behavior. It's a power play. Hopefully, men don't feel bad about some of these revelations because feminine and masculine behavior aren't tied to gender, even though our society has attempted to marry them over the centuries. As human beings, we all utilize both feminine and masculine behavior in various ways throughout our lives. Why? Because if we don't, we'll perish individually and collectively. We must utilize both the feminine and masculine to survive on the planet. Actually, it's impossible not to do so since we are inherently composed of both energies. It's not even optional; therefore, we should drop the stereotypes we've been fed over the years and realize the truth of how we move and operate as people. The fact that we've tied femininity to power should make the transition easier for men who've grown up in a modern culture.

It's important to note that nowhere in this description have we mentioned the feminine being associated with being submissive. It should be apparent why that's the case at this point, but for clarity: anyone who truly possesses power has zero need to be submissive. The feminine uses its power to achieve its goals and objectives and has zero interest in applying that power to the will of others. But more importantly, when we look at femininity, it can't submit, which is why we have a separate designation for submission in this book. Anything as intentional as power, magnetism, attraction, and accomplishment is far too intentional to submit to anything or anyone. Both the feminine and masculine simply do what they do and are not necessarily interested in how or to what they are applied. They are tools for accomplishment. As stated earlier, they are modalities of behavior based on the flow of energy. This must be clarified because of the misconception that femininity is associated only with women and that women in their feminine are naturally submissive beings, which can't be further from the truth.

So, what are some practical feminine (i.e., power-based) behaviors that we can observe? Examples include being reserved in speech because not revealing what you know or how much you know is a powerful action. Most people tend to speak about what they know very loudly and frequently. This is why the ability to keep a secret is so highly valued, while gossip is considered cheap and wasteful and something practiced by those who don't see their own self-worth. Trust in relationships is often built upon each person feeling they can be vulnerable with one another and knowing their communication won't be shared with others. We fully expect credit card companies, credit agencies, and government organizations won't share our personal data and information with the world. We expect them not to sell it even though we know our information is valuable in the marketplace. There are sayings about the wise person who knows a lot but shares practically nothing. Other terms for private are discreet, secretive, special, exclusive, reserved, hushed, separate, independent, and confidential.

Beauty and the art of making oneself beautiful is a feminine expression. Taking time to focus on making oneself look appealing based on cultural standards of beauty is powerfully feminine. It's not easy to ignore a beautiful person. They almost demand our attention regardless of what we're doing at that moment. There have been many close call car accidents as a result of a driver's attention being caught by a beautiful and attractive person. Advertisers use beauty as a way to get people to buy their products, look at their magazines and movies, and think highly of their brand. The art of sacrificing one's time and energy to the point of cultivating their beauty is a thing to behold and is a powerfully feminine expression. Other terms loosely associated with beauty are grace, symmetry, charm, elegance, glamorous, agreeable, friendly, safe, wonderful, inviting, nice, kind, and shapely.

The art of beauty leads us to attractiveness and magnetism. Because we find ourselves drawn to beautiful people and things, it can also be said that we're attracted to them. They are magnetic in nature; although we have no intention of directing our attention toward them, they somehow pull us in. That's magnetism. It's powerful and effective at shifting the physical reality around us. It can change people's minds and focus, bringing attention and favor and drawing in energy. Again, most people would love the ability to draw people to them just by them walking into a room or being present. Many of us would value the attention and focus of others, including our spouse, committed partners, and friends. Magnetism allows us to do that. Synonyms for magnetism and attractiveness are seductive, hypnotic, irresistible, enchanting, captivating, mesmerizing, pulling, inviting, appealing, and alluring.

As noted earlier, the ability to conserve is a feminine expression. Conserving one's energy, money, time, and physical effort is powerful, especially when most people end up working harder than they'd like just to receive nominal returns. It's our dream as human beings in Western culture to do minimal work and receive maximum payout. We'd all like to work four hours a week and receive fifty thousand dollars a week in return. Why? Because we don't want to expend our energy on things we don't want to do;

therefore, power is the ability to save our energy for what's really important to us—fun, health, actual emergencies, family, love, life, etc. People who are conservative have no interest in showboating or displaying themselves as an indication of their worth or value. They simply want to be as efficient as possible and complete the task at hand. That's it. No frills, no acknowledgments, nothing extra, no wasted time. This is a powerful feminine display of energy and behavior. Someone who practices conserving can also be described as reserved, stable, steady, or constant.

It should be noted that everything that is saved or conserved doesn't fit under the definition of conserving. When we say conserving, we're talking about things of value (i.e., energy, money, and assets) that can be used at a later time if needed. Hoarding, for example, is not considered to be conserving and is a form of wasting. Keeping too many things can be counterproductive when not done so consciously and therefore has the effect of taking away one's power.

We can see how the trait of conserving energy can also translate into nurturing as a feminine expression, where mothers need to conserve their energy for themselves and their babies and children. A breastfeeding infant is going to take milk (i.e., energy or resources) from their mother; thus, she must have the skill of reserving her energy or the child will suffer. You can't nurture others if you don't have anything to give them. Nurturing is literally taking a piece of yourself, reshaping it, and giving it to others so they can grow and benefit in some substantial way. Nurturing is a material exercise where substance is the ultimate measure. The giving of time and energy and resources is key. Other terms that align with nurturing are supportive, caring, nursing, nourishing, increasing, tending, raising, rearing, developing, and bolstering.

Again, conserving energy while at the same time getting work done is a feminine trait. Maximum work accomplishment with the least amount of physical output is a powerful expression. That's why bank robbers show their guns to the teller and the teller subsequently gives them the money. They know the power potential associated with the gun; thus, no demonstration of force is necessary. In addition, we could associate the power of prayer, ritual, ceremony, and spirituality as feminine. The concept of prayer, whether one believes in it or not, is that you ask for something to be done and it somehow magically gets done. For example, you ask a higher power—or the power within yourself—to keep your child out of harm's way while they are deployed overseas during their military service and they come home safe and sound. Or, you pray that your son wins his court case and doesn't have to go to prison and he ends up winning. Again, whether you believe in prayer or not isn't the point; rather, if someone is able to tap into a higher power or metaphysical force such that it affects the physical reality around them, we consider that as an amazing show of power and a feminine expression. It's the least amount of physical work with the maximum physical outcome. In addition, for those who have taken the time to understand, practice, and tap into a metaphysical force such that they have enough mastery over it to use it as a tool for accomplishment in the physical world, this is quite the feat. If most people could pray themselves into riches, they would do it. If they could use prayer to solve their problems, they certainly would. This suggests tapping into these metaphysical abilities is elusive to most people, just like beauty and wealth.

Creativity is a feminine expression as well. The ability to solve any problem or challenge with the resources that are available is incredibly powerful and valuable in our society. The ability to turn an ugly environment beautiful, which is actually an artistic expression, is also feminine—the ability to make a way where there apparently is no way. The ability to tap into your intellect and understand how (i.e., strategy) to move forward in life to achieve the success you desire is powerfully feminine indeed. Imagine combining some of these feminine traits, like the ability to see how to get things done for success and the ability to be reserved in speech (i.e., not telling anyone what you know), while conserving your energy, money, and resources until you have what you need to actually implement this strategy. Now, we have someone who's maximizing their feminine energy to make major moves in the world and in their life. The idea that only masculine expression gets things done is a misconception. Another way to look at creativity is the ability to synthesize and coalesce information and things into a functional and unified whole such that they have an effective function in the world. This is essentially fusion, integration, and unification.

What do we get if we combine the feminine attributes of beauty and conservation? We get royalty. Someone who looks amazing and therefore attracts attention and favor as well as someone who keeps to themselves and focuses on what's important to gain the desired results. Isn't that what a queen is? Beautiful, rich, and reserved in speech and behavior. No one ever questions her power, understanding, or intelligence. She's not just an outward presentation, but also an information treasure chest.

These are a few examples of feminine expression and energy, but there are many more. You can take the time to see where you use power in your life to affect your reality.

The Masculine Precept

If feminine behavior can be characterized by power, masculine behavior can be characterized by its complement—force. What is force? Force is the activity of directing energy outward toward the objects we are attempting to affect. Again, both power and force have energy as their essential component, but what differentiates them is how the energy is channeled and directed. I'm redefining power from the internalization of energy and force to the externalization of energy. As stated before, masculine behavior is defined as any act that utilizes force to affect objects and our environment. In other words, masculinity is the act of effecting change through force, while femininity is the act of effecting change through power.

If the feminine is attractive, then conversely the masculine is repulsive, which sounds bad, but it's the truth. The compliment to attractiveness is repulsion, which is defined as the act of moving objects away from you (i.e., the source of the repulsion). It's simple, right? Attraction draws objects toward you, while repulsion moves them away from you. Stated differently, femininity utilizes attraction to affect and change the environment, while masculinity utilizes repulsion. If we can really embrace these simple definitions of the masculine and feminine behavior dynamic, we'll be able to have clarity on what's really happening inside of our relationships. Let's look at some examples. If someone enters a room with a knife and begins swinging wildly, they are clearly acting in a repulsive manner and are further inside of their masculine behavior. If a linebacker tackles the quarterback during a football game to stop him from throwing a touchdown, they are functioning in their masculine. In this example, the quarterback is repulsed by the linebacker and will either attempt to throw the ball before the linebacker gets to him or he'll try to run away from him. The linebacker is forcing the quarterback to move away from his desired location on the field and throw the ball before he'd like to throw it. This is force. Staying with this example, if the linebacker can't get to the quarterback and the quarterback has plenty of time to throw the ball, he may have to deal with a different set of elements affecting his decision-making process. Maybe he decides not to throw the ball because the safety is sitting back in the middle of the field just watching the quarterback's movements. If the quarterback decides not to throw the ball because he fears the safety will make a move to intercept it, it's not force affecting the quarterback, but rather the power of the safety. It's the safety's speed and reactionary potential that's causing the quarterback not to throw the ball. In both of these hypothetical situations with the safety and linebacker, the effect is the same, but the major difference is that the linebacker's influence on the quarterback's decision-making process is obvious, while the safety's influence is subtle. This is an important distinction between masculine and feminine behavioral displays. Masculine behavior is fully available to the five senses, while feminine behavior requires an intuitive sense to recognize. Force and power work in the same way. Anyone who utilizes force to influence others can be clearly seen because of their overt nature, but power tends to be covert. This is why the feminine gets the label of being mysterious—although its capabilities are respected, they aren't necessarily obvious. The masculine is quite the opposite and gets the label of being loud, obvious, rude, and repulsive. Now, we can see how these energy dynamics begin to play out more clearly in relationships and society as a whole.

This is the challenge with recognizing institutionalized racism, classism, and sexism because they are power-based institutions; in other words, they don't overtly oppress or discriminate, but instead do so covertly. This also holds true for individuals who abuse others in relationships by using their power inside of the relationship to intimidate. It's not so obvious when this happens compared to someone who is using physical force to affect the behavior of others. For example, a dictatorship is an oppressive governmental regime that uses military force to oppress its people and dictate their behavior. The oppressive techniques are evident—torture, killing, jailing, and overt threatening of the populace. On the contrary, a corporatocracy is a power-based governmental structure that can mask itself as a democracy. It's harder to see because it doesn't have to force anyone to do anything, but instead controls the flow of capital and resources through complex laws and systems designed to be (1) hard to understand, and (2) difficult to navigate even with an understanding of the system because of the requirement to have significant resources and networks to successfully navigate it. If people were to try to criticize the corporatocracy, they would be simply told, "We all have equal opportunity to be successful." It would be hard to argue against this rebuttal because you're not being forced to do anything. You could walk into a bank and apply for a loan. You could apply for a passport, start a business, choose to work or not work, relate with anyone you'd like, start a family, team up with a thousand people and protest for a cause you believe in, or anything in between. It's the feminine form of oppression and it utilizes a power structure that is difficult to identify.

If a man approaches a woman in a bar and offers to buy her a drink, he is using force to attempt to acquire sex from her and is therefore in his masculine. The fact that he approached her is a masculine behavior. The fact that he utilized force in the form of money to influence her judgment by buying her a drink is also a masculine behavior trait. If he initiates conversation with her and maintains that conversation, he is once again utilizing force and therefore acting inside of his masculinity. Let's take a moment to note two things: (1) the fact that a man is utilizing force to obtain sex from a woman doesn't negate the fact that she may be using power to gain the same thing or more, like marriage and long-term commitment; and (2) functioning inside of the masculine or feminine has nothing to do with functioning inside or outside of one's moral judgments. Both forces can be operating at the same time, and when they do, we can have what they call mutual attraction if both people are interested in one another. In terms of morality, we need to understand that it's a judgment on someone's behavior and doesn't affect the quality of behavioral expression. After we classify a behavior as masculine or feminine, we can subsequently label it as moral or immoral, good or bad, effective or ineffective, or whatever we wish. That's a totally different conversation and we shouldn't get sidetracked by the variety of judgments we'll see for every single behavior.

Let's look at a few more examples for clarity. If a man and woman are naked in the bed and the man leans over and kisses the woman, he's in his masculine behavior pattern. He forced himself upon her in hopes of initiating sex. At the same time, she may have utilized her power to attract him into using force by the way she was laying, moving, or looking at him. Again, both of these behavior dynamics can be in play at the same time. If two people roll over at the same time and start kissing and rubbing each other, they both used forced to initiate sex. If both parties are in agreement with how they are forcing themselves upon one another, we have a consensual and intense sexual interaction; however, if one disagrees on how the other is forcing themselves, we don't have consent. For example, both parties could throw themselves upon one another, but let's say the man is trying to force the woman to give him oral sex, but the woman insists on kissing or having him suck her breasts instead. In this case, the sexual encounter could end abruptly. What we have here are two people in their masculine behavior dynamic, thus potentially causing things not to work out. When someone applies force upon someone else, there must be a level of receptivity at play in order for it to work. In other words, there must be a force-power dynamic somewhere within the mix. It should be noted that two people utilizing power solely to attract sex will never have sex. These are people who may even like each other and be attracted to one another, but because neither of them wanted to force themselves on the other, the sex never happened. This happens all of the time in courting and dating where both people are in their feminine behavior and therefore nothing happens. We also see this in dating where a man may see a woman he's attracted to in the grocery store and smile at her. She may smile back because she's also attracted to him, but neither approaches the other. Why? Because they were both in their feminine energy. They may have even gone home and told their friends they saw someone they were super attracted to, but they didn't approach them. When this happens, people often feel regret, disappointment, and shame about not having the courage to possibly meet the love of their life.

These examples give us a bit more insight into the masculine as the overt, physical initiator in life. Again, without both the masculine and feminine, nothing happens, but it's important to understand the dynamics at play. The same goes for the feminine, because if the feminine wasn't attractive to the masculine, the masculine wouldn't have a reason or desire to act upon it.

Let's look at some examples of masculine behavior. When someone is bold with their communication, they're in their forceful masculine behavior. Words are used to influence people in our society. Often, we attempt to influence someone's beliefs or convince them to show us favor in some way. Bold and aggressive communication is also used to show our discontent with a situation or for negotiating a better position in our lives with those who could adversely affect us. We see this with businesses who aggressively market their products and services. They're invasive to our private life with advertisements on our social media, in our email, and through telemarketing efforts over the phone. In most cases, these are sales pitches that we don't want to hear or see but are forced to because of our participation in society. For example, driving down the street will force you to see billboards, signs, and people in costumes on the side of the road advertising various products. It's almost unavoidable. When you go to the grocery store, there's usually a special offer stand or sign from a company wanting you to taste test their product. This is called force, and communication is a big part of it. From one perspective, this overcommunication is the opposite of privacy and reservation. Privacy is keeping things to yourself and is feminine, while making things common, public, ordinary, and open is a masculine behavior trait. What's also masculine is the act of gossiping, revealing information, uncovering what has been hidden, lecturing, and preaching.

Being rough and repulsive are also expressions of force. No one wants to be around someone who's rough or someone they're repulsed by; even though these qualities sound off-putting, they're obviously necessary. These qualities are the foundation of security and protection. It's less likely someone will assault a home or family if they know there are rough characters residing in the house. It's less likely a nation will be invaded if they know they will be repulsed by a military force greater than their own. It's less likely you'll be bullied in school as a child if you carry some repulsive character traits. You may find yourself more successful in sports or in business if you can show a rugged toughness about you that could translate into strength. Again, when we engage in the exercise of combining masculine traits (i.e., bold communication and repulsiveness), we find people who negotiate the cheapest deals on car and home purchases. We also find people who others choose to leave alone for fear of experiencing their wrath up close and personal. Many bosses and managers have a combination of these traits and end up getting maximum effort from their employees because no one wants to be called out for inefficiency or poor performance. We definitely see these traits in the military, whether it's basic training or special forces training, where individuals must be pushed beyond their comfort zone if they're going to reach the levels they need to be at for success in their new roles. We can also see these traits in teachers of martial arts, ballet, and gymnastics. Some of the roughest communicators use these behaviors to squeeze maximum potential out of their students. Other terms synonymous with roughness are objectionable, disagreeable, undesirable, off-putting, distasteful, abhorrent, unsightly, obnoxious, gross, and revolting.

If conserving is a feminine trait, using is a masculine trait. One person is saving money, while the other is spending it. Again, using money to obtain things is a show of force and a way to get what we want and influence our environment. We often see this in politics and business where someone uses their money to buy influence when making laws or setting policy. One rule of business and entrepreneurship is to not save money when you make it, but instead to reinvest it back into the business. It's a constant circulation of resources in an attempt to obtain credit lines to use for purchasing supplies or for marketing purposes. This is the ultimate show of force in the world in order to grow one's business, gain clients, and secure investors. The difference between "use" in this example is that it's not a waste. Using means taking money and resources and spending them to obtain something of value or to effect change. Just throwing resources away without obtaining anything for them isn't using them—that's wasting. Other terms for use are spend, release, capitalize, exhaust, work, bestow, exercise, apply, employ, exploit, manage, manipulate, and utilize.

The act of nurturing is a feminine trait, which essentially means to increase or add to. In this case, the masculine compliment would be to diminish or decrease. This may sound foreboding and negative until we need to remove an obstacle from our path or put a hole in a mountain so railroad tracks and roads can be built. The concept of diminishing can also be applied to addictions, habits, and certain types of behavior. Again, basic training is not only about teaching new military personnel specific rules of conduct, but also about eliminating bad habits people picked up through civilian living like waking up late, needing more personal space than necessary, speaking in a disrespectful manner, being out of shape, refusing to cooperate with others or work as a team because of petty differences, overcoming fears, and eliminating negative thoughts about personal capabilities. The very act of working out on a daily basis is about eliminating excess body fat. Dietary programs like veganism, vegetarianism, paleo, and keto are really more about elimination and decreasing the foods that aren't healthy. Bruce Lee is quoted as saying, "It's not the daily increase but daily decrease. Hack away at the unessential." The entire concept of minimalism is about decreasing unnecessary things in life on a daily basis. It's a show of force to go from two hundred and fifty pounds to one hundred and ninety. Other terms for decrease are diminish, moderate, taper, subdue, depreciate, and reduce.

If prayer is a feminine trait, organizing spiritual beliefs into a system or religion is a masculine trait. The metaphysical connection to spirit and the ability to use that connection are inherently elusive; thus, the masculine role would be to turn those metaphysical capabilities into a science and something that can be repeated. Spirituality is feminine, but science is masculine. Connecting with spirit (i.e., what can't be seen) is feminine, while connecting with nature and the material realm (i.e., what can be seen) is masculine. The spirit can't be identified with the five senses, but the laws governing the spirit can be put into a book and studied and applied. We can see how these two qualities of energy expression can work together in harmony and produce spiritual systems and experiences that are beneficial to all and practical to use. However, we can also see what a potential imbalance may look like where the spiritual laws become detached from the spirit—in other words, no real connection is experienced by those observing the practice. The opposite effect is possible as well, where spiritual connection is only understood by a few with no real way to transfer that knowledge to others, thus leaving the masses disenfranchised.

The ability to break things down into their individual components and analyze them is an act of force as well. This means analysis, segregating, breaking down, partitioning, and scrutinizing are all masculine traits as well. It's of critical importance to be able to break down our reality into its components so they can be understood and studied. This can lead to finding chemical elements that can cure diseases and improve health outcomes, like extracting serums from a certain species of mushroom or the latest craze using cannabidiol (i.e., CBD oil) as a cure for many medical conditions. Additionally, breaking things down allows us to understand how to build them better. We've seen this with studying the bodies of the deceased to better understand surgical procedures, bone repair, and organ transplants. Other terms for analysis and breaking things down are interviewing, inquiry, investigation, and testing.

These are just a few examples of masculine behavior based on the concept of force.

Androgyny Unmasked

The gender energy that sits apart from both masculine and feminine is called *androgyny*. As a gender energy, androgyny simply describes energy in a peaceful state. It literally sits still, allows itself to be at rest, and has no inclination to flow in any direction outside of environmental dictation. Therefore, it doesn't attract masculine or feminine energies to it and simultaneously doesn't repel them either. It's essentially indifferent; as such, it is willing to move in whatever direction it's influenced to move. This androgynous gender energy is necessary in order for us to have a relationship with ourselves as well as higher orders of nature. It allows us to simply be (i.e., exist) without experiencing a pull or interference from others. It's almost like existing in the void or in a floatation tank. In addition, the androgynous nature allows one to align with the organic flow of the natural forces around them, which means there will be a seamless synchronicity with their environment.

Without the gender energy of androgyny, it will be impossible to truly love and connect with others because we will not know ourselves deeply enough to practice self-love, which is a prerequisite for loving others.

However, there's another important aspect of androgyny, which is the tendency to gravitate toward truth and understanding based on what's needed at a particular time. This means androgyny is an energy that allows individuals to flow in the direction of knowledge, wisdom, and experience based on how and where it's occurring in the environment at any particular time. For this reason, androgynous individuals tend to be quite intuitive and can tap into the deeper meaning of life and purpose. They can also understand the path to success because they allow themselves to be receptive to that knowledge. Compared to the feminine individual who tends to stay attached to their current source of information, position, or ideology, or the dominant person who may insist on creating their own path, the androgynous person follows the path of truth and least resistance, which will eventually lead to the answers they seek. The prerequisite for their posture in these circumstances is an understanding that wisdom through intuition is an innate trait that all humans possess, and that the solutions to our problems are inherent to the problems themselves. In other words, life cannot present you with a problem without also simultaneously presenting you with the solution, as they are two sides of the same coin. In this way, we can say that the androgynous energy involves a form of either dominating or submitting to one's environment such that the truth, path, and light can be revealed and subsequently followed effortlessly. They have no desire to create a new way forward (masculine) and have no desire to stay with the old way (feminine); therefore, they are free to flow toward "the" way when it's presented.

Lastly, androgyny as an energy tends to flow toward existing imbalances in the environment. As a result, individuals carrying androgynous energy will naturally gravitate toward where their talents or skills are needed. Yes, it's going with the flow, but energy naturally flows toward voids, lowest points, areas of sickness and ill health, chasms, and weak links. This means an androgynous person might find themselves interacting with those who are in need of their talents, without having to make any effort to seek out those individuals.

It can be said that everything we need is all around us; however, we need to allow ourselves to "see" those resources since they may not be obvious to the naked eye. For example, someone lost in the woods may starve to death because they don't know what is edible versus what is poisonous. The reality is that they are literally surrounded by food, water, and sustenance. If they know the sources of food in the woods, they can use masculine energy to find and harvest those items. Once they find those food sources, they can use feminine energy to maintain their presence. Regardless, androgynous energy is also required to guide the individual to flow toward what they need. We've all experienced the feeling of being lost and then miraculously ending up where we needed to be. Some would call that luck, but for the sake of defining these gender energies, we'll call it being receptive to the androgynous energy within.

Summary of the Gender Energies

If we were to summarize the gender energies of masculine, androgynous, and feminine, we could say the masculine goes against the grain, the androgynous goes with the flow, and the feminine holds its position or attaches to what it desires. The diagram below illustrates how these energies impact a ball on a slope.

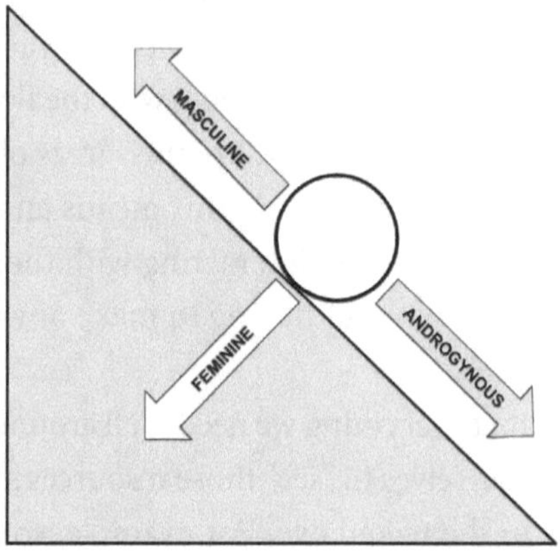

Contrary to popular belief, when a ball flows downhill when it's on a slope, it will function in an androgynous nature. This behavior has mistakenly been labeled as feminine. The truth is that no effort is being made for the ball to roll down the hill; thus, its energy output is close to zero (although this isn't technically true). What we know is that the feminine is the compliment to the masculine, which means their energy expenditure will be equal yet applied differently. In this case, the feminine is using its energy to hold its position, thus resisting the force pulling it downhill. Theoretically, this is the same amount of energy the masculine uses to go against the grain and move up the slope. The actions of the masculine are just that—to go against the grain, to create its own path, and to move in opposition to environmental forces.

The Archetypes

Before we leave the discussion of gender energy, we need to introduce the concept of archetypes in order to give us a deeper understanding of the differences between masculinity, femininity, and androgyny. We can break down the masculine, feminine, and androgynous gender energies into nine total archetypes.

Masculine Archetypes:

- SOLDIER – The aspect of masculinity in charge of engaging in physical conflict, protection, sacrifice, and risk-taking. It's the keeper of courage and all things martial in nature. Its role in the relationship is that of the protector.
- LEADER – The aspect of masculinity in charge of organizing, managing, leading, and taking accountability. It's the keeper of rational thinking, prudence, and responsibility. Its role in the relationship is that of the husband and father.
- NEGOTIATOR – The aspect of masculinity in charge of communication, trade, business, negotiation, and political discourse. It's the keeper of assigning value and exchange. Its role in the relationship is that of the financier and facilitator.

Feminine Archetypes:

- CONSERVATIONIST – The aspect of femininity in charge of mental toughness, feminine intuition, conservation, and consistency. It's the keeper of cycles and formal structures with healthy limitations. Its role in the relationship is that of the witch.
- DEVOTEE – The aspect of femininity in charge of commitment, duty, nobility, nurturing, dedication, and belief in one's partner. It's the keeper of secrets, confidentiality, and devotion to one's partner. Its role in the relationship is that of the wife and mother.
- LOVER – The aspect of femininity in charge of pleasure, romance, sex, ease, and beauty. It's the keeper of joy, artistic

expression, and submission. Its role in the relationship is that of the lover.

Androgynous Archetypes:

- PEACEKEEPER – The aspect of androgyny in charge of being detached from the world as needed as well as finding inner peace within themselves and apart from people or circumstances. It's the keeper of the ability to create one's life and flow into any gender energy as needed.
- MONK – The aspect of androgyny in charge of gaining mastery in any area of life, being purpose-driven, deep thinking, seeking counsel and guidance, and intuition. It's the keeper of wisdom and knowledge. Its role in the relationship is that of the wise elder.
- VISIONARY – The aspect of androgyny in charge of creativity, freedom, strategic thinking, wealth, exotic experiences and expressions, and love. It's the keeper of optimism and the ability to accomplish anything in the world. Its role in the relationship is that of the adventurer and strategist.

Emotions as Energy

We've covered some great information about the masculine and feminine as well as their essential components of force and power. We've also established that energy is the primary determinant from which behaviors are categorized as either masculine or feminine—but what is energy, exactly? Although we've been extremely technical up to this point (out of necessity, as these concepts must be firmly grounded), this book is really about relationships and how we can make them better and understand them more. When it comes to human behavior, energy is simply expressed through our emotions, which are described as our state of mind that is subsequently translated into how we feel in our body. So, we have a certain state of mind which dictates how (i.e., the direction) the energy in our body moves, in turn affecting how our body feels. The stimulus for our state of mind is how we interpret what we observe in our environment, including the thoughts and images in our heads. This interpretation is translated into the movement of energy, which feels a certain way, thus prompting us to describe that feeling as a particular emotion. For example, if I observe my girlfriend breaking up with me and I interpret that breakup as tragic, my energy might be overwhelmingly drawn toward my heart, which feels like the emotion of heartbreak and extreme sadness. Or maybe I just got a raise at work, which I interpret as an acknowledgment of my worth, causing the energy in my body to flow to both my heart and head and filling me the feelings of pride, happiness, and elevation. These are just a few examples to help us understand what we mean when we say energy. Energy moves throughout our bodies based on our mind state, and the feeling of the energy coursing through our veins, organs, and major pathways is what we call an emotion.

Taking it a step further, we can also change how we feel inside by changing our mind state. For example, if I start feeling high about myself, the energy will move accordingly; thus, I'll experience feeling pride and happiness. Energy really does follow the mind. We learn this in our energy work courses, where we're told to focus our minds on the parts of our clients' bodies where we want the energy to flow. We also see this when we're children. When we fall down and hurt our knees, our mother tells us to look at her and don't think about it (i.e., focus on it) and it will feel better.

It's the same exact concept. Like Kenya K has always said, "What you focus on expands."

When we look at the components of WILL, ENERGY, FORCE, PEACE, and POWER relative to masculine, androgynous, and feminine expression, we get a relationship where WILL is the initiator of energetic movement, which eventually impacts human behavior as either masculine, feminine, or androgynous in its expression.

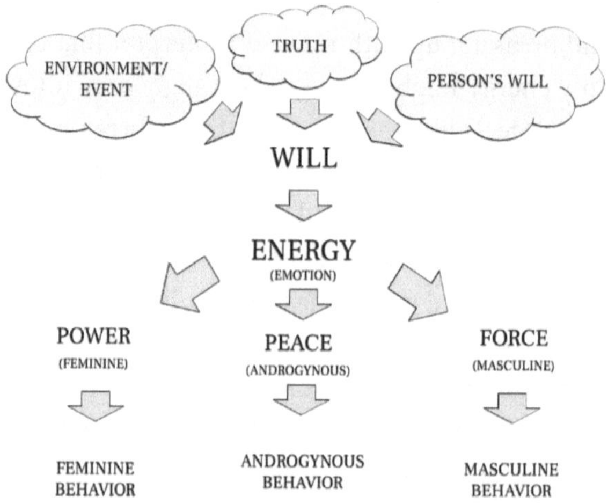

Combining Gender Energy & Position-Roles

We've clearly defined the position-roles of dominance, neutrality, and submission as well as the gender energies of masculine, feminine, and androgynous, leaving us with the question of how they all come together in a practical way. Let's refer to their combination of possibilities as the Gender Energy-Position-Role Matrix, or GE-PR (pronounced "jep"-"ur") for short.

How does this affect our relationships and how do we know how to leverage these dynamics to improve our interactions with our partners? First, here are the nine possible GE-PR combinations: (1) masculine-dominant, (2) masculine-neutral, (3) masculine-submissive, (4) feminine-submissive, (5) feminine-neutral, (6) feminine-dominant, (7) androgynous-neutral, (8), androgynous-dominant, and (9) androgynous-submissive. Let's discuss what each of these combinations looks like.

Masculine-dominant is defined as doing physical work at your own will, where you are the primary beneficiary. In other words, these actions are not subject to the will, orders, or behest of another person. They initiate the action and move in the direction they desire without the need to answer to anyone else. In the example above, the quarterback is the masculine-dominant and calls the plays he desires (unless the coach has that role). The quarterback dictates where everyone goes on the field and controls when the ball is snapped. A related example is a woman whose boyfriend lives with her in a house she owns. He lives with her, but she does the work to support the house financially. In order for him to stay, she expects him to contribute equally financially, do chores to maintain the home, and follow her rules inside the home. In this case, she is the masculine-dominant because she is the primary worker in the house while also establishing her will and desire as a condition for him to stay. In this case, he would be in a submissive role within the relationship.

The archetype that falls under the masculine-dominant category is the LEADER. The LEADER is a masculine-dominant archetype that desires to be in the controlling and accountable position for everything they're involved with. It leads others by being present with them and offering proper examples and guidance for their success. It's masculine in that it initiates its own activities, and it is dominant in that it imposes its will upon the people and partners it's leading.

Masculine-neutral is defined as the propensity to move and initiate change while also being disengaged from engaging with others. This is the true definition of a person on a mission who starts out alone and only accepts help (i.e., lessons, support, and guidance) when it is freely offered. An example is a high school athlete who goes to the gym every day to work out and improve their athleticism for football. The student is in their masculine energy because they are initiating and performing the workouts they dictate. They are in the neutral position because they are alone, they don't require guidance from anyone, and they are not looking to guide anyone else. No one is ordering them to work out and they are not subject to others for their performance. If they decide to stop working out today, no one would say anything about it. The masculine-neutral is that stereotypical wandering warrior who walks the countryside alone in search of their own life, free from governmental dominance or the agendas of others.

The SOLDIER is a masculine-neutral archetype that sacrifices itself on behalf of its mission and goals. It's the personal risk-taker. It is masculine in that it initiates all of its activities, and neutral in that it doesn't desire the guidance of others while simultaneously having no interest in having others following them.

Masculine-submissive is defined as doing physical work at the will and behest of another person, who in most cases is the primary beneficiary. As they're in their masculine energy, they will serve in an initiatory capacity and not wait for direction. With that said, they will be initiating activities that are in service to the will of someone in a more dominant position. A classic example is a wide receiver running a route that's been dictated by the coach and quarterback. When the quarterback snaps the ball, the wide receiver will run the route dictated by the quarterback and put themselves in position to make a catch. They may have to improvise or change routes, which means the quarterback will have to change where they throw the ball, but that's still in alignment with what the quarterback desires. Another example is a factory worker who is in charge of assembling and installing the gear boxes on cars as they come down the assembly line. The worker is in the masculine because they are initiating and performing the construction of the gear boxes. They are in the submissive role because they are doing their work at the will of the company who pays them. If they do not perform at a certain level, they will be reprimanded by their superior, who is an agent of the company.

To determine whether you're in a submissive position, ask yourself the following question: Who has the authority or right to pass judgment on my activities in a way that would have to at least be considered, if not outright followed? A relationship example is a woman who owns a condo outright and has her boyfriend living with her for free. She works and pays all of the bills. She is in the masculine because she is doing the physical work to maintain the home. She is in the submissive role because she is supporting her boyfriend's lifestyle. In this case, the boyfriend would be the feminine-dominant because he's allowing himself to be supported in alignment with his will and desire. He's in the feminine in that he's not working, but holding firm in his position of allowing himself to be acted upon and taken care of. He is the dominant in that his girlfriend is carrying out his will of being supported and cared for.

The archetype that falls under the masculine-submissive category is the NEGOTIATOR. The NEGOTIATOR is a masculine-submissive archetype that appreciates the value of material resources, social and business networks, and effective communication. It affects others through its logical view of life. It's masculine in that it initiates its own activities and submissive in that it's dependent upon the buy-in of others.

Feminine-submissive is defined as conserving oneself at the behest and benefit of others. The feminine-submissive takes part in activities that increase their power for the sole purpose of that power being utilized by a dominant person at a later time. An example is someone who has been given money to go to the spa and have their nails done, get a massage, and get a facial. These are activities that will increase their energy and improve their health and beauty; however, it's the dominant person who plans to capitalize off of that improved health and beauty. Maybe they are going to a sales event and the dominant person feels having a beautiful person with them will assist them in gaining favor with executives. Another example is a young man who's living with his mother, but doesn't have a job and doesn't do any work in the house except when told to. He's in the feminine because he isn't initiating any physical work or activity in the home. He's in the submissive because he's subject to his mother's rules and orders as long as he's living in the house.

The archetype that falls under the feminine-submissive category is the DEVOTEE. The DEVOTEE is a feminine-submissive archetype that focuses on its duty to the relationship as being a proper and consistent representative at all times. It's the nurturer of the family. It's feminine in that it holds its ground while waiting to be acted upon, and it's submissive in that it yields its will to those who offer it growth, protection, love, and honor.

Feminine-neutral is defined as the propensity to hold firm in one's position while also not being particularly interested in engaging with others. In this case, although one is steadfast in their desire to hold firm in their present position and standing, they are open to being engaged by others when approached or when the situation naturally presents itself. Because they are neutral, they are inclined to function based on what their environment presents to them rather than an independent goal or objective. Their neutrality also has them moving independently of others without a real need to connect with people in any capacity. A classic example is the elderly lady who lives her life to the best of her abilities while not expecting or hoping for any support from others even though she would welcome it. In this example, she's been doing things for so long by herself that her mindset is that she will handle all of her business on her own. Her femininity is established in the fact that she is going about her routine without stepping outside of her boundaries or comfort zones. She's staying within what's already established and most effective, which is different from the masculine that desires to challenge established boundaries and obstacles.

The archetype that falls under the feminine-neutral category is the CONSERVATIONIST. The CONSERVATIONIST is a feminine-neutral archetype that utilizes its inner power to achieve success in life. It's consistent, reserved, and respectful of minimalism as well. It's feminine in that it holds its ground while waiting to be acted upon, and it's neutral in that it doesn't have an affinity to connect with others in a submissive or dominant role.

Feminine-dominant is defined as conserving oneself at their own will and benefit. The feminine-dominant person takes part in activities that increase their power solely for their own benefit and use. An example is someone who makes sure they get ten hours of sleep each day as well as plenty of rest, water, and high-quality food. This will increase their overall health and give them more energy to use at their discretion. Another example is someone who decides to travel to see the world for their own benefit and experience. Traveling allows them to expand their understanding of various cultures, languages, and food and have a better awareness of people in general. This activity yields personal improvement on both a mental and intellectual level. A further example is a young lady who lives in her boyfriend's house on the condition that he supports her and allows her to have the freedom she desires. She's in the feminine because her boyfriend is pursuing her and she's in the dominant position because she's setting the conditions by which the relationship operates.

The LOVER is a feminine-dominant archetype that appreciates beautiful expressions and romance. It does not only appreciate beauty, but also utilizes it to gain favor in the world and to affect and influence those around it. Beauty is an art and skill and is a powerful force in the universe. It represents symmetry and the coming together of various forces in our environment. The LOVER is also flexible and pliable, which allows it to not be stuck in any situation. It's feminine in that it doesn't allow itself to be moved until it chooses to. It holds its ground until it's ready to move.

Androgynous-neutral is defined as not having a preference for any gender energy or position-role. It's the ability to be at peace without playing any role within the GE-PR Matrix. Its only desire is to relate to itself, and although it has the ability to play any position within the GE-PR Matrix, it's not attached to any of them. It can release its masculine or feminine energy without feelings of anxiety or regret, and can do the same with the dominant or submissive position-roles. This is a genuine state of neutrality that's demonstrated by actual action and activity.

The archetype that falls under the androgynous-neutral category is the PEACEKEEPER. The PEACEKEEPER is an androgynous-neutral archetype that utilizes its ability to detach from people, ideologies, beliefs, addiction, and material attachments in order to achieve success in life. It remains in a state of peace and calm in the face of adversity and can flow into what it needs to be in any moment. Its androgynous gender energy is that which stays neutral in situations but becomes either feminine or masculine as needed, and it's neutral in that it has no particular need to follow anyone's will, including its own. Its neutrality allows it to remain solo and without the need to connect with anyone else.

Androgynous-submissive is defined as flowing with whatever is presented without needing to hold firm in its current position or to initiate change. In addition, there is a readiness to serve once the opportunity or need presents itself. The combination of androgyny and submissiveness makes these individuals both approachable and amenable. What makes them unique is that their submission comes as a result of what's needed as opposed to what they will or desire. This is the role of the androgynous energy, which flows toward situations most in need of fixing and rebalancing. Once these individuals have arrived in their new environment, they submit to addressing the needs of where they're at. In this way, their submission is based on the environmental need rather than to a person, per se.

The MONK is an androgynous-submissive archetype that prioritizes wisdom and understanding over logic and reason. It is purpose-driven and goal-oriented. It's androgynous in that it flows and interacts naturally and organically with its environment based on the quality of that environment, and it's submissive in that it looks to share with others its deep insights and intuitive knowings. The MONK looks to share its knowledge of how things could be better in order to restore balance and health to whatever situation it finds itself in.

Androgynous-dominant is defined as flowing with whatever is presented without having to hold firm in its current position or to initiate change. There is also a readiness to teach and lead others as the need or opportunity presents itself. The androgynous energy will push these individuals toward areas where their talents can be most utilized to bring about balance, health, and order. Once they are situated, they will tend to dominate the environment, including the people around them, as a prerequisite to bring about the change required to restore that environment.

The VISIONARY is an androgynous-dominant archetype that focuses on creativity, invention, and strategic ways to solve problems. It's the purveyor of wealth and freedom of expression. It's androgynous in that it flows with the energy and environment for which it is a part of, and it's dominant in that it takes charge in order to carry out its solutions to restore balance and order.

You may notice there is some overlap in the examples given above. That's to be expected because we're never only in one dynamic, but consistently balancing and displaying all nine dynamics at all times. However, our goal is to identify the primary dynamics playing out between people in order to avoid confusion.

These dynamic combinations lay the foundation for why and what we choose for ourselves in relationships. Some people prefer to be in the submissive role while others prefer dominance. Some people would rather be in their masculine while others prefer the feminine or androgynous energy. And even with our preferences, we find situations where we may enjoy specific dynamics with certain people because we trust them to bring out a particular talent within us or to give us a certain experience.

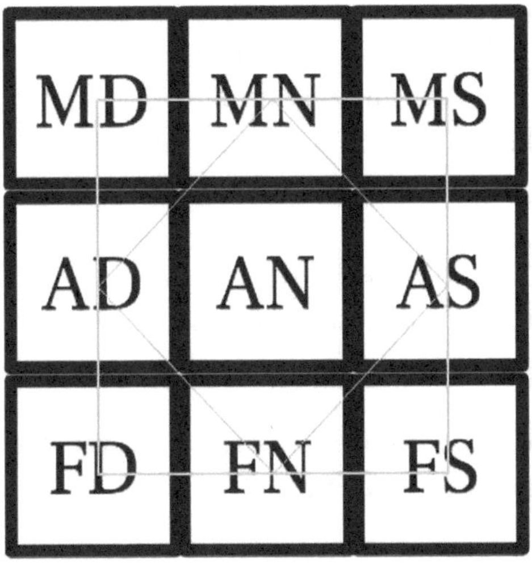

Now, let's take a look at the GE-PR Matrix in order to see how everything relates to each other.

When we lay the GE-PR Matrix out graphically, it looks like the diagram above, where MS is masculine-submissive, MN is masculine-neutral, MD is masculine-dominant, AD is androgynous-dominant, AN is androgynous-neutral, AS is androgynous-submissive, FS is feminine-submissive, FN is feminine-neutral, and FD is feminine-dominant. This is actually a mathematically precise diagram, but there's no need to delve into this further in this book. The point is that we have the androgynous-neutral in the center acting as a balancing force between an equal number of feminine and masculine gender energies located at the bottom and top of the diagram, respectively. The androgynous-neutral element is also the center piece of the dominant and submissive position-roles, as represented by the diamond and square outlines.

In summary, we have:

- LEADER – Masculine-Dominant
- DEVOTEE – Feminine-Submissive
- SOLDIER – Masculine-Neutral
- CONSERVATIONIST – Feminine-Neutral
- NEGOTIATOR – Masculine-Submissive
- LOVER – Feminine-Dominant
- MONK – Androgynous-Submissive
- VISIONARY – Androgynous-Dominant
- PEACEKEEPER – Androgynous-Neutral

When we replace the GE-PR designations with the archetypes, we get the following diagram.

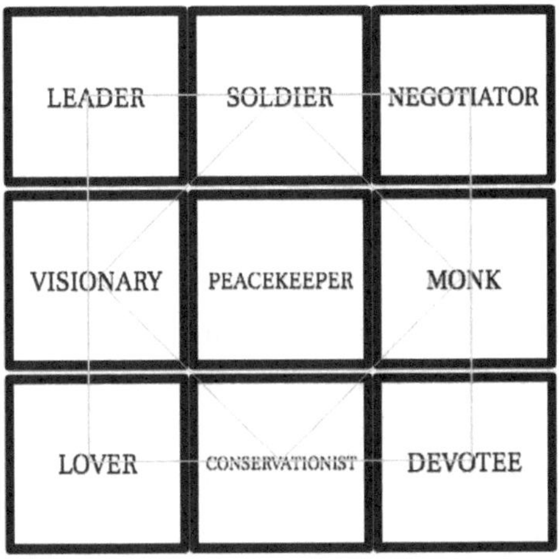

Again, these archetype designations are not random, but rather mathematically placed. In any case, we can observe how the archetypes and GE-PRs are all related, both in their natural states and relative to one another. This diagram also helps us rank each individual GE-PR relative to the others.

First, let's lay out the GE-PR rankings and later we'll explain how we arrived at that conclusion.

- The most submissive feminine archetype is the DEVOTEE.
- The most submissive masculine archetype is the NEGOTIATOR.
- The most dominant feminine archetype is the LOVER.
- The most dominant masculine archetype is the LEADER.
- The most masculine neutral archetype is the SOLDIER.
- The most feminine neutral archetype is the CONSERVATIONIST.

Now, let's rank the archetypes by gender energy and position-role, individually.

- The most masculine archetypes are the LEADER, SOLDIER, and NEGOTIATOR equally.
- The most feminine archetypes are the DEVOTEE, CONSERVATIONIST, and LOVER equally.
- The most dominant archetypes are the LEADER, LOVER, and VISIONARY equally.
- The most submissive archetypes are the DEVOTEE, NEGOTIATOR, and MONK equally.
- The most neutral archetypes are the PEACEKEEPER, SOLDIER, and CONSERVATIONIST equally.
- The most androgynous archetypes are the VISIONARY, PEACEKEEPER, and MONK equally.

That's all of them. So, how do we use this information exactly? We would just say it can be useful when analyzing relationship dynamics between people. When we see two people together who have the most masculine and feminine archetypes, respectively, we can predict they'll be a good match and simply need to work through aspects such as principles, wants, needs, likes, and dislikes, and not who should be initiating versus who should be waiting for direction. When we see the most submissive archetype aligned with the most dominant archetype, we'll be able to assume who chooses who in the relationship and whose will and direction will most likely be followed. The same holds true when we see two people with the most dominant archetypes together in a relationship. We can accurately predict they will bump heads about who's in control versus who should follow. If we see two people with strong feminine archetypes together, one of their challenges will likely be who should initiate communication, sex, and activities within the relationship. Conversely, if two people who have strong masculine gender energies are together, both people might feel they're in charge of initiating sex, communication, family meetings, etc. and that their role is being cannibalized by their partner.

These designations simply give us a starting point for problem-solving inside the relationship and are not meant to be the only tool used to assess challenges.

What is Choice?

In this chapter, we'd like to make a distinction between choice and desire. Choice is a feminine and submissive expression of mate selection, while desire (i.e., masculine choice) is a masculine and dominant expression for selecting a partner. That's right—the feminine and masculine go about mate selection differently, which shouldn't be a surprise. Not only do they go about it differently, but they are also each seeking something different, even though it might not be obvious from the outside. As with most of our discussion up to this point, we'll largely stay away from assigning masculine to males and feminine to females because it's critical that we understand the underlying energy at play so we can assess which energy dynamic we're functioning from.

The two components of choice are (1) having a vision of what we'd like to experience in a relationship, and (2) picking a person that fits into the vision. This means if you don't have a vision for what you want in a relationship, you're not choosing. First comes the picture, and then comes the process of filling in the pieces of that picture. That's the technical definition, but let's back up a bit.

Who chooses in relationships? Like, who actually opens the door for relationship connection to take place? Is it a mutual thing where both potential partners simultaneously choose one another? That's the fantasy, right? We both caught eyes and it was love at first sight. We both had a vision of what we wanted in a relationship and each person fit perfectly into that vision. We couldn't stop staring at each other and then we just came together and embraced for what seemed like hours. I guess it happens that way sometimes—my wife and I met on a blind date. I would say our attraction was mutual and simultaneous; however, she chose me first. It took me a week or two to choose her back. But the mutual and simultaneous attraction where both people feel the same way at the same time is mostly an anomaly in our culture. Generally, why we're attracted to someone and when we're attracted to them varies from person to person. What usually happens is one person sees the other first. Maybe they spend some time stalking and observing before allowing themselves to be noticed. Even when two people meet in person for the first time, the desire to be together isn't usually equal. Usually, one or both people need time to warm up to each other and see what they like and don't like. They need to visualize what things would look like in an actual relationship. Then come the dates where they get to be in one another's presence and feel things out or look for flaws or signs of who this person really is. That's where we make sure they don't share certain qualities that our ex-partners had. Or maybe one person knows from the moment they see someone that that's their wife or husband. The point is that in most relationship scenarios, one of the two people actually liked the other person first. In other words, someone made a conscious decision that they wanted to be in a relationship with this specific person. They decided in their mind, heart, and body that this is the person for them.

An example of choice is knowing that you want a huge wedding, beautiful children, a house with a picket fence, anniversary celebrations, and plenty of extended family gatherings during the holidays. This is the vision (i.e., component #1). The experience is a done deal in your mind already; you just need someone to share it with and help bring it into physical reality. Thus, all that's required is to find a partner that fits into that vision (i.e., component #2). When you meet someone who you can see playing the role of partner in your vision—meaning they have the look and feel of the person in your vision—you choose them. This is a case where you must choose them because they can't be attracted to the vision in your head. They can't see what you're thinking, but they can be attracted to you as a person. This helps clarify why the feminine aspect is so particular when it comes to choosing a potential partner and why others often have trouble understanding their selection because it's entirely in their mind. Only she can see how everything matches and fits together. When someone approaches her and says, "He seems like a nice guy," it doesn't mean anything. Sure, he might be a nice guy for someone else's vision, but not for mine. This makes "choice" a very specific and meticulous process. It's not random or haphazard at all.

Submissive Choice

Do all of us choose in the same way? Maybe, but there are some very specific factors we need to observe in our mechanisms of choice. Remember, we're saying that choice has two components: (1) a vision, and (2) the person who fits into the vision. When we look at choice from the standpoint of position-roles (i.e., submissive or dominant), we can observe that the submissive person is looking to "level up" in their life to a place where the dominant person currently resides, or at least to where the dominant person can take them. They are looking to gain skills, guidance, or insights, or awaken something within that the dominant person has already demonstrated within their lives, even if they aren't totally aware of this on a conscious level. Thus, the submissive is looking for a dominant to serve in order to gain what they desire (i.e., a vision of where they see themselves). The dominant person has achieved success in a particular area of their life and understands that success, cultivated talent, or skill represents an attractive force in the world that will draw people to them. Confidence is a vortex of attraction. Beauty is a vortex of attraction. Power is a vortex of attraction. Demonstrated force is a vortex of attraction. Financial, business, athletic, and academic achievements are all vortexes of attraction. Physical stature and symmetry are both vortexes of attraction. Sexual prowess, skill, and vitality are vortexes of attraction. These vortexes attract those who desire to experience the energy created by that vortex. This means the submissive person seeks the dominant person in order to be in that vibration. They're attracted to it. In other words, the submissive chooses the dominant they'd wish to connect with, follow, submit to, and learn from. Again, only a person who chooses to learn from someone will actually be able to learn and benefit from what the teacher has to offer. As the expression goes, "You can bring a horse to water, but you can't make it drink." There is no leadership, guidance, or dominance without an eager and willing participant—it's the student who must choose the teacher. The teacher is always ready, but students come and go based on their readiness and interest.

Submissive Person —> CHOOSES —> Dominant Person

Feminine Choice

Let's move to gender energies (i.e., masculine and feminine). The masculine by nature is outwardly focused. Its mission is to deal with the world, subdue it, and reshape it into its likeness. The masculine utilizes force to do this. It seeks its validation through finding that which it can shape and alter to its liking. Thus, the masculine is consistently looking out for that which it can engage with. It's a master of the physical environment and is desirous and eager to interact with it. The masculine is open in mind, spirit, and body to the material and external world. This contradicts a popular narrative that the masculine's heart is closed to feeling; quite the opposite is true when the masculine is in a balanced place. The masculine's heart is open to the world, but tends to be cut off from itself, meaning it resists going into the depth of its own inner world and feelings and is thus closed to the inner self. The masculine loves faster and harder than the feminine because it must be able to connect with all physical reality if it wishes to have any kind of mastery over it. The feminine, on the other hand, is internally focused and doesn't have the same comfortability with the outside world. The feminine is focused on remaining inward and living within its heart and mind; however, it also seeks the external world experience. The feminine is the master of the internal world, including visions, imaginings, memories, strategies, creativity, and artistic expression. The feminine crafts entire worlds from the inside out; thus, it's not as familiar with the outside world and needs time to connect to it. Therefore, the feminine is the gatekeeper's choice because its ability to choose is limited to what it can understand and connect with.

The feminine has a healthy fear of the physical world and desires a guide in the form of the masculine offering its energy in exchange for its guidance and protection on the journey. The feminine seeks an understanding of money, assets, resources, land, people, communication, and a variety of physical phenomena. It seeks an understanding of how to interact with people in a social and business setting. It seeks to understand the limits of the physical body and what it means to extract maximum pain and pleasure through it (i.e., childbirth). It seeks to understand the depths of the world and the truth of the physical phenomena around it. It seeks these experiences through the masculine and thus chooses a guide in the form of a partner or mate to do so.

When we say choice, we mean the feminine is looking to choose a specific person that matches their vision. That's why we say the feminine is the chooser of a mate or partner. This isn't true for masculine energy, which is looking for a specific experience but is more open to exploring that experience with a variety of people. For example, if the feminine desires to be with someone for their financial acuity, their choice of qualified partners will be far fewer than that of the masculine. It will take more than just someone with money because the feminine will still need to connect to their heart and body and they'll need to match their internal view of what that experience is supposed to look like.

The masculine, on the other hand, can connect to almost everything in the world. The masculine loves all, both broadly and generally. The feminine loves few deeply and specifically. The masculine loves the world. The feminine loves the self. The masculine runs from the self while embracing the world; the feminine runs from the world while embracing the self. Thus, the feminine is the primary chooser because it takes longer to choose. The masculine has already chosen. The feminine is a more specific chooser in an effort to bring pieces from the material, external world to fit into and match its internal world view. The masculine stays ready while the feminine needs time. This is what we mean when we say the feminine is the chooser in relationships.

Feminine —> CHOOSES —> Masculine —> To Gain a Physical Experience (Finding the World)

The primary choosers in relationships are feminine-submissive. The primary responders (rejectors or acceptors) to begin choosing are masculine-dominants. Let's not make the mistake of assuming that only women are the choosers in relationships because that's not what we're saying at all. When a human being chooses someone they'd like to be in a relationship with, they are choosing from either their feminine gender energy, their submissive position-role, or a combination of the two. Thus, both men and women choose partners in relationships depending on which part of the GE-PR they're operating from.

Let's make sure we're clear that choosing a partner takes place in the mind, meaning we must decide that we're going to engage with someone. We actually say, "Yes" in our head to connect with a specific person. The heart and body must also be aligned with our choice, but the mind is the ultimate determinant of whether we choose someone or not. The physical attraction might already be there, and the emotional connection might be there as well, but the mind is still the gatekeeper to the initial choice.

Masculine Desire (i.e., Choice)

If the feminine and submissive are the primary choosers in relationships, where does that leave the masculine and the dominant? Do they choose? Not exactly. They may "choose back" once chosen, but the masculine mainly has desires it wishes to fulfill. Desire means the masculine is looking to experience a certain quality of feminine energy so that it can get closer to its inner self. In theory, the masculine has already mastered the world and isn't looking for support in that continued exploration. It's the inner world that's the challenge. Again, the masculine gender energy is detached from its inner world, but it desperately seeks this world. The way the masculine ultimately discovers this world is through experiencing love with the feminine. How does the masculine attract the feminine? By creating an environment that matches what he believes to be her inner vision of what she wants to experience in a relationship. If he wants to experience the nurturing love of the feminine, he creates an environment where that can be facilitated. He dresses himself up as the type of man who needs, desires, and deserves nurturing. He provides the house where nurturing can take place. He demonstrates that he values nurturing through his actions and speech. This activity attracts a nurturing person to him, who hopefully chooses him, which subsequently allows him to choose back. This is how the masculine chooses (i.e., desires).

Masculine —> DESIRES —> Feminine —> To Gain a Feeling Experience (Finding the Self)

The masculine desires to feel true love in its heart and soul. It desires to experience empathy and connect with the feelings (i.e., pain and pleasure) of others. It desires to experience true freedom from responsibility and the ability to enjoy the bounty of the world. It desires to experience true inner power that is sourced from its soul as opposed to external phenomena like money, position, or title. It gains these experiences by loving the feminine and learning to connect with it in a sincere and organic way.

The two components of desire are (1) creating an environment that attracts a partner who can support you in how you want to feel, and (2) "choosing back" the partner who's drawn to that environment in order to intensify the feeling you're seeking.

Dominant Desire (i.e., Choice)

The dominant, on the other hand, seeks acknowledgment and witnessing, which it can only get from the submissive. Again, it's not specific to who acknowledges it as long as those individuals carry a certain quality of energy. For example, if I want acknowledgment of my mastery of spiritual information, I'll take all comers. Fill the arena up with thousands of people wanting to hear my sermons and buy my lectures. I don't even have to see their faces. Would it feel good if all those attendees were drop-dead gorgeous and geniuses in their own right? Of course. The higher the quality, the better it feels to the ego. But at the same time, let's admit that the arena being full is at the top of the hierarchy. It's just like we said—quantity over quality for both the masculine gender energy and the dominant position-role person.

Dominant —> DESIRES —> Submissive —> To Be Witnessed and Acknowledged

So, this is our complete breakdown of choice and desire. If we align women with femininity and submissiveness, we can see why women are the primary choosers in relationships. They need to be able to connect with specific individuals in order to carry out their vision of what a relationship looks like. Another way to say it is that the feminine prioritizes quality over quantity. In addition, we can see why choosing a partner would be a complicated endeavor for women as well, and why they may go back and forth at times about who they're choosing. This is because they sometimes lack the clarity of "sight" (i.e., being able to know who a person really is). In other words, they're not always sure about who they're choosing, what that person has to offer, what they're about, or how to relate with them. Who tends to change their mind about having sex right before the act of sex happens? Usually, women. Why? Because they're not always clear on who they're with. It takes them time to get to know a person before they can choose them. Because what they thought they saw doesn't always turn out to be true and accurate. Because once they get physically closer to someone, they're able to see them better. Or maybe they were unsure all along and rushed into the sex before they were aligned in mind, spirit, and body with their choice. Maybe they felt bad or ashamed about not being sure faster. Maybe they didn't want to lose the man they're vetting because they're taking too long to decide. What if he's the one and she loses him because she took too long to make a choice? What if someone else is also choosing him and she loses out? It happens to all of us. It's not easy.

Sometimes, women don't realize they haven't fully chosen their particular partner yet and end up moving forward with the relationship even though they are unsure about things. In other words, choosing a partner (being aligned in mind, spirit, and body) isn't a simple process. It takes patience, prayer, and trust. It also takes a certain level of surrender to the choosing process. Choosing a partner is an initiation in and of itself for women, who must learn to align their inner vision with their feminine intuition to ensure the person they're considering is the right fit. This means changing the vision up just a bit because of the type of vibration it's giving, which may lead a woman to attract the wrong type of person. It may also illuminate the fact that she is not aligned with her vision—meeting the right man causes her to reflect deeper on herself and realize she's not the woman in her own vision. Somewhere along the line, she may have lost sight of what she needed to do for herself in order to keep the dream alive. Like we said before, it happens to all of us.

This leads us to a challenge the masculine may have in either choosing back or selecting someone who fulfills their primary desires. If you're being chosen by someone who's unsure, it might not feel quite right to you as a man. Sure, you may engage in sex or develop a friendship with her, but you're not feeling certain about an actual relationship. Maybe that woman becomes hard to lead or to be present with because she hasn't totally chosen you yet, which means you won't get the feeling and experience you're seeking as a man. You won't get focused love from her, which in turn will leave you feeling empty. She hasn't totally bought into the idea of being with you and trusting your leadership. Her uncertainty about you and the relationship is reflected in her lack of receptivity to you; thus, there is a disconnect between the two of you. This can lead to blaming and finger-pointing about how each person isn't showing up, and a lack of awareness that the problem could be that a legitimate choice hasn't been made by the feminine or submissive principle. The initial choice, which we call The First Choice™, is the critical foundation for any relationship. It comes down to the following: (1) Did you actually choose to be with me in your mind, heart, and body; and (2) What is the vision that you want me to be a part of? Anyone who's going to be in a serious relationship must be clear on these things if they want success. If you didn't choose me, I can't realistically choose you back. If you didn't choose me, you won't be able to fulfill my desires and the relationship won't work. I'll feel the need to go outside the relationship and choose someone else. Either that or my desires won't be fulfilled; thus, I'll still be longing for that void to be filled within me. We see this happen often in relationships and we usually don't have an understanding of why. Instead, we cast blame on one another for why our relationships don't work, without realizing that the relationship didn't stand a chance from the beginning. Since a legitimate choice was not made or the First Choice™ wasn't acknowledged or discussed, neither person could fulfill their roles in the relationship.

This is no different from a student giving a teacher a hard time in school or not being able to pick up the lesson. They simply haven't opened themselves up to the teacher enough to receive instruction. There's still resistance, lack of trust, and uncertainty, which lead to an ineffective and perhaps an adverse relationship. Maybe the student isn't one hundred percent committed to learning a particular subject or discipline. We see often where students change their major after the first year or before they graduate. They never made the choice. Or maybe they made a choice but were not clear on where they were going with it (i.e., no vision). After they graduated, they never ended up doing anything with the degree. We've all seen the difference between those who make a choice with conviction, confidence, and surety versus those who waver. Remember: no vision, no choice.

The same holds true for the masculine and dominant principles of desire. Is the man clear on what he desires to experience, or is he resistant to it? Has he set up the proper environment to be chosen by the woman carrying the quality of love he's looking for? Does he personally carry the vibration of a man who can be loved in that way? Many women complain that he won't open up in relationships—that he won't trust her to love him, take care of him, and protect his feelings. Why? Because he's not fully clear on what he desires from the feminine principle or he's completely oblivious to what he's seeking on a subconscious level (which most men are). He could think he's seeking sexual gratification when his spirit is really seeking the experience of feeling from the inside out. This means feeling love and acceptance of the total self and loving his shadow and inner demons just as much as his light side. Maybe he's just imitating what he sees other men doing or what he's seeing in movies and is not aware of what he really and truly wants for himself on the inside. This means he doesn't have a true desire or at least isn't aware of what his true desires are. When a man doesn't realize he's on a journey to experience the deep inner parts of himself, he becomes incapable of knowing who can give him the experience he so desperately seeks.

To make matters even more complicated, once men start to feel their inner self, it can be quite scary. Feeling your inner power for the first time can be painful or at the very least uncomfortable. Feeling love for the first time can be intimidating. The feeling of energy flowing through new channels in the body along with new sensations in different organ systems can catch men off guard, especially if it's their first time going there. This is essentially him feeling new and different emotions than what he's ever experienced to this point in his life. These new feelings can also manifest as pain, which is a part of the journey; when he feels pain, he may blame her for bringing out those feelings instead of understanding he's the author of his own experience. She's just enabling his desire, but he's the master of fulfilling his desire, which includes feeling pain, heartache, and emotional uncertainty that emanates from the inside out. She can go through the same thing where the physical, real-world experience of love brings out emotions that make her feel uncomfortable. One example is living with a man and having him evoke emotions that you previously didn't have to face as a woman. Being challenged physically to provide for and please him can be a shock to the body and mind and may cause you to question yourself—am I capable of being a wife? It may cause you to question if he was the right choice because things just don't feel right. They're not supposed to feel right, but instead give you a feeling that you've never experienced before—an experience you could only imagine.

The masculine is seeking to connect with its heart, but to do so it must open up to the feminine, become one with it (surrender), and allow it to guide him through the abyss. The feminine is seeking to connect with body and mind, but to do so it must open up to the masculine, become one with it (be vulnerable), and allow it to guide her through the wilderness.

Androgynous & Neutral

Both the androgynous and neutral energies fall outside of choice and desire for others. The androgynous gender energy doesn't have any polarity; thus, it's not drawn to anything outside of itself. As such, it also doesn't magnetize or attract anything to it. The feminine gender energy is in a constant state of attraction and magnetization in search of its complementary energy. The masculine is also on this search; however, it doesn't rely on attraction, but rather its aggression to fulfill its inner need and longing to match up with its complement. The androgynous gender matches with itself and environment and therefore is complete. Its preference is to be by itself and simply flow with what the environment provides. The neutral position is similar in that it's not seeking connection with a compliment. It's essentially in a state of rest and therefore does not want to connect with others but would rather rely on itself to supply what it needs for fulfillment and fortification. Another way to say it is that the neutral person is choosing themselves only, which falls outside of the choice paradigm. In short, they fall outside of the Choice and Desire Paradigms but are open to being chosen or desired.

Part 2: The Love Expressions

The 9 Expressions of Love

A love expression is simply an indication of how we show our love to our partners. It's a series of behaviors and functions we exhibit that indicates we love someone. Even more, it's our signal that we are in fact loved by the person who's demonstrating that particular love expression toward us. We have a total of nine love expressions and each will be detailed in this chapter. These expressions can be used to determine where you are on the GE-PR Matrix: masculine-dominant, feminine-dominant, androgynous-dominant, masculine-submissive, feminine-submissive, androgynous-submissive, masculine-neutral, feminine-neutral, or androgynous- neutral.

The premise is that all human beings desire to connect with a certain type of person or have a certain quality of experience inside of their relationship, but in order to attract those experiences, they must demonstrate a behavior that's attractive to their potential partner. For example, if you want to date a certain woman who's young, beautiful, and vibrant, you might have to shower her with material things or make her feel special and unique in some way. Conversely, if you'd like to date a man who's sexually powerful, you might have to show him the highest level of deference and respect. If you want to marry someone who'd be a great spouse, you might have to demonstrate an ability to be present and tuned into their daily needs. In other words, we are embodying the expression of love required to attract the relationship experience we're looking for. It's true there are certain love expressions that come more naturally to us and we'll use those whenever we can, but the question isn't what is comfortable or natural to us. Instead, it's about what the people we're attracted to want from us. In addition, as our relationship needs change over time, we'll find ourselves using different love expressions to gain those new experiences.

The foundation for why we might naturally choose one love expression over the other has everything to do with our values as well as cultural and astrological influences governing when and where we were born, our relationship history, what we've observed with our parents and other close friends and relatives, etc. Sometimes, those natural love expressions get us exactly what we desire in our relationships; other times, we need to make personal growth changes and learn a new way to express love to others. Is it a violation of ourselves to love someone in the way they want to be loved when it doesn't come naturally to us? No, because it's about doing right by someone because we love them. We love them in a way they desire to be loved because we want to show up for them in the best way possible. We want to do whatever is required to make them happy, which in turn should make us happy if we truly love them.

It must first be noted that what we expect from others in how they show us love isn't necessarily how we show them love. For example, someone may express their love through a show of power but expect to be showered with money and material comforts as the love expression they desire. One of the greatest misconceptions in relationships is our belief that others want what we want and feel how we feel. We all want to be acknowledged and loved differently, and that's perfectly normal.

What we must also understand is that human beings go through changes over time and often have varying needs. That means we may look for multiple love expressions from various people over time in order to get different needs met. It's rare that we would want to express our love in only one way over the course of our entire lives, even if it's within a single relationship.

In addition, how we ultimately show love to someone is solely based on the judgment of that person. In other words, you can't say how you show up for someone else; it's really up to them to make the final judgment as to how you're showing up. You can think you're showing up as someone who's financially supportive as your primary expression of love, but they see you as a sexual goddess. Or maybe they acknowledge that you're doing some things financially for them, but it's not enough to really be considered as financial support from their perspective. The person receiving your love will be the judge of what your love is to them; thus, as we define the 9 Expressions of Love, we'll explain them from the perspective of what others desire to experience from you. This is important because Person A might experience Jenifer as a sexual goddess, but Person B sees her as a sexual lame. As we indicated in our book *UPLVL Communication™: The Ultimate Solution to Save Relationships and Eliminate Hurtful, Damaging, & Meaningless Arguments*, there is no absolute truth. Everything is subjective.

The 9 Expressions of Love

- Power Love – Love based on prioritization, conserving energy and resources, and deferment
- Manifestation Love – Love based on specialness, prioritizing material comforts, and communication
- Freedom Love – Love based on encouraging freedom of movement, creativity, and expression
- Support Love – Love based on physical presence, protection, and support
- Soul Love – Love based on a common mission and the desire to elevate the soul
- Devoted Love – Love based on devotion, dedication, and consistent performance of duty

- Crown Love – Love based on adherence to protocol, morality, and purpose
- Romantic Love – Love based on specialness and the public appearance of the relationship
- Womb Love – Love based on physical passion and sexual connection

As we examine these love expressions, we should understand that there are two sides to them. Side #1 denotes the behaviors and activities we exhibit in a relationship that we expect to be taken as our expression of love, while Side #2 describe the behaviors we look for in others as an indication of their love for us. As mentioned above, we'll discuss the 9 Expressions of Love from Side #1: how we express our love for others. It should be noted that Sides #1 and #2 can be the same thing, but not always. Many of us desire to be loved in the same way we love others, but we're going a bit deeper here. The truth is, throughout our lives, we desire to be loved in a variety of ways. We also desire to love others in different ways.

Power Love

Power Love is in play when we want to be loved for our ability and willingness to (1) prioritize our partner and the primary relationship over everything else, including our own individual needs; (2) maintain high levels of discretion and privacy; (3) push to protect the relationship by adding a formal structure to it (i.e., marriage institution); (4) prioritize our partner's sexual satisfaction above our own; (5) prioritize saving, accumulating, and reserving resources (i.e., money) valuable to sustaining the relationship; and (6) tap into spiritual forces on our behalf.

Some of us show our love by demonstrating to our partners

that they are the absolute center of our world and by ensuring their happiness, comfort, and fulfillment is what brings us joy. It's a show of inner fortitude and an ability to deny our wants and needs in deference to others. My happiness in the relationship is a result of you being happy. It's not just us prioritizing our partners and putting them first, but also the intermittent demonstration of denying our personal pleasures and comforts and, in some cases, our own happiness in deference to theirs. This is the ultimate demonstration of the power our partner wields in our world when we're able to defer so strongly that we potentially deny ourselves in the process. It's the ultimate show of respect to the importance they play in our lives.

We know this may sound extreme, but we defer in this way all the time. This is the kind of deference we see paid to Michael Corleone in "The Godfather" by his soldiers, family members, and workers. The respect (i.e., love and appreciation) shown for Michael acknowledges his role in creating a fulfilling life for his family and associates. It acknowledges the importance of the sacrifices he's made on their behalf and how he's protected them over the years. They show this deference by prioritizing Michael's needs and orders over their own. They literally drop whatever they're doing at the moment in order to protect and serve Michael. It's not just being done out of duty, but also out of sincere love and appreciation for who he is and what he represents to them. He's literally creating a better life for them. He's literally protecting their lives on a daily basis. He's literally giving them access to a lifestyle they could only dream of. His life and work are so critically important that they love, respect, and almost worship him as the man he is—a man of immense power. This display of love (i.e., Power Love) by his family and associates is how you love people of power. It's what they expect and it's what they need in order to continue to influence your life in profound ways. It's from the heart and can be felt by those receiving it. It can be imitated, but it can't be faked because the cost of Power Love is too great. No one is willing to sacrifice their own happiness unless they truly have a profound love for the person. A person would have to truly find love in the act of deference.

I remember when I was a part of a spiritual community and we had a hierarchical government with a king and queen at the top. I loved the information, teachings, and work the community was doing for the world. The king was the author of our entire spiritual philosophy and I saw him as a man of great power. I still do, actually. Anyone who could channel such brilliance and teach it, while being a representative of those teachings, was a powerful man indeed. Whatever he and his family needed, I made sure to offer it when I could. When he came into town, I would volunteer to drive him around the city, buy him food, arrange accommodation, etc. It didn't matter what I had going on with work or family; I would defer to him when he came to town. That was how I showed my love and respect for him. No one made me do it. I had a deep love for him and who he represented and that was the source of my actions. My love expression for him was Power Love.

On the surface, denying ourselves may sound extreme, but it's what we do every day without realizing it. We practice it in other areas of our life when we go to work, feed our children, pay bills, do chores, file our taxes, cook dinner, wash dishes, and so on. These are all activities we mostly don't want to do. We'd much rather be on our phones, playing games, watching television, having sex, relaxing on the beach, or sleeping. These are activities we would outsource if we had the resources to do so. No one desires to drive an hour and a half through traffic to work every day, but we do it because we feel we must. We deny our desire to stay in bed or quit our jobs out of deference to bill collectors, those who depend upon us, and the pressures and demands of life. In addition, we defer to our own desires. Many of us want to have a lifestyle of comfort, live in nice houses, and drive beautiful cars, so we defer our comfort (i.e., being lazy, etc.) and go to work and school. Why? Because it feels good to work every day? No. Because we're putting our dreams and long-term wants and desires first. Some of us do the same with physical fitness. Instead of eating muffins and drinking vanilla milkshakes every day for breakfast and sleeping in, we get up and go to the gym. We eat salmon and veggies instead of pizza and garlic knots. That's self-denial and deference in action. See? It doesn't sound so bad when you do it for something you love, right? That's Power Love.

If I practice this kind of self-denial in my life for something bigger and better, I just might consider it the ultimate show of love for myself. I'm managing my diet and activity every day because I love myself. I'm saving money and investing because I want the best for myself in my later years. I'm continuing my education because I respect my potential too much to allow it to go to waste. Wouldn't it make sense then that when I see someone sacrificing for me in the same way, I interpret it as them showing how important I am in their life? I'm just as important as your nice car, a big house, savings account, and healthy body; thus, you making the same quality of sacrifices for me as you do those things means you love me. Is that a stretch, especially since I'm willing to deny myself in the same exact way? All this means is that if you love and truly appreciate me, you'll be willing to prioritize me above everything because I provide that kind of value to you—Power Love.

This translates sexually as well where we're willing to defer our pleasure, albeit temporarily, for our partner's sexual pleasure. Our partners are clear about their sexual satisfaction and getting them pleased first and foremost is the priority. If they aren't pleased, the sexual interaction is a missed opportunity. This is actually a form of compersion where your own sexual satisfaction is intricately linked to theirs. The sound of your orgasm and climax is a sign that we have reached the heights of our physical and spiritual love connection, and that is pleasing to me. This dynamic is common in formal (i.e., contracts) submissive and dominant relationship structures, where the dominant person receives pleasure first. The submissive only receives pleasure when the dominant person says it's time.

Again, this may sound a bit extreme, but in our tantra and sexual education classes taught through the Progressive Love™ Academy, we teach men to bring women to full pleasure first due to her need for more stimulation and build-up. It's about taking your time as a man because your climax is almost guaranteed, whereas hers isn't. In addition, when she reaches multiple orgasms during sex, it increases your pleasure as a man exponentially.

NOTE: Often, those who desire to be on the receiving end of Power Love won't necessarily acknowledge the need to be pleased first because it can be viewed as selfish, but it's how they really feel. In truth, there are those of us who get offended when we don't climax during sex, while others are more understanding. They get especially offended if their partner climaxes but they don't. These are also people who desire to have a partner who expresses their love via Power Love, which translates into "me first." It's best not to look at this as something selfish, but simply as a preference.

Another aspect of Power Love is proactively asking our partners what they need, as well as simply doing what needs to be done. This is a major part of expressing Power Love, where the anticipation of our partner's needs is also a priority. For them to have to come to us and ask is considered as a failure in some cases. Going back to the example from The Godfather, the anticipation of Michael's needs when he comes to town is the ultimate show of respect and love for him. He shouldn't have to ask for a meal, protection, or a ride. If we love our partners in this way, we should anticipate their needs and provide for them. People who like to receive Power Love don't necessarily want to ask for what they need, and fully expect their partners to learn about them in that way.

There's also a spiritual aspect that can be left up to your individual belief systems, but it's believed that some of us are able to tap into a spiritual power and ability that can be used to affect the reality around us. An example is when women pray for their loved ones to recover from surgery. Again, some may believe in this type of thing, while others do not. For those who do, Power Love is also expressed in utilizing this ability on behalf of one's partner in order to improve their lives or help them in some way. Trust us—there are people out there who truly value the power of prayer and the utilization of spiritual forces. This was big for me in my marriage with Kenya. I wanted her to utilize her spiritual tools and abilities to help the family in all ways possible—our children's health, my career, our sex life, buying a house, etc. Again, you have to align this work with your belief system to see if it's something that may benefit you.

Power Lovers tend to be feminine-neutral like the CONSERVATIONIST, expecting their partners to initiate sex and anticipate their needs. Their partners ask what they need when they're not sure; otherwise, they fully expect them to know their needs in advance and anticipate them whenever possible.

MASCULINE DESIRE PARADIGM: Later on, we'll talk about the Masculine Desires, which highlight what both the masculine gender energy and the dominant role-position look for in a relationship connection and why. When a masculine or dominant person chooses someone back who Womb Chooses them, it's called fulfilling Power Desire, which is one of five masculine desires. In other words, they are choosing back this person because of the way their love (i.e., ability to focus on them and bring intensity) ultimately makes them feel—powerful.

Do you practice Power Love with your partner? If you answer YES to most of these questions, you might express your love in this way and have CONSERVATIONIST tendencies when it comes to relationships.

1. Do you defer to your partner without them having to ask you?
2. Do you prioritize consistency of action in the relationship?
3. Do you ensure your partner has a formal relationship structure (i.e., marriage) they're comfortable with? Does this relationship structure provide clear boundaries and limitations?
4. Do you keep details of your relationship private (i.e., minimal social media, minimal public interaction, etc.) and separate from others as a critical component of relationship success?
5. Do you anticipate your partner's needs as a normal part of maintaining a relationship?
6. Do you value long-term, committed relationships as a necessity for your partner's happiness inside of the relationship?
7. Once you've found a routine your partner likes, do you

ensure that routine is maintained over the long term without major changes?

8. Do you prioritize your partner's sexual pleasure above your own?

Before moving on to the next love expression, let's look at a few more considerations. First, Power Love isn't about abuse and shouldn't be used as an excuse to endure abuse—whether physical, emotional, or otherwise. Although the recipients of Power Love tend to be feminine-dominant, domination doesn't equal tyranny. A sane person in a dominant position only uses that position to teach, guide, love, and build their partners up. A true dominant understands limitations and practices self-discipline and control to ensure everyone is safe. Anyone practicing Power Love should feel loved and appreciated at all times; otherwise, they should leave the relationship. It's counterproductive to be in a situation, giving your all, and not receiving love in return. The standard for whether you are receiving love in return should be how you feel. Ask yourself the following questions: Does this feel good to my spirit? Would I support my children in being in this same love dynamic when they become adults? Am I growing from this relationship or am I regressing? The answers to these questions can be your guide to whether your Power Love expression is being appreciated and properly reciprocated. Just like anything else in life, it's up to you to be the manager of your own happiness. Never put your happiness in the hands of others. Never justify consistently not feeling good as something necessary or normal. Anyone offering Power Love to others is a gift, and their love offering is worth more than gold. Always use discretion.

Lastly, remember that everyone has different levels of what they desire inside of their relationships. This also includes what each person may expect inside of a love expression. In other words, you may express Power Love inside of your relationship and it is sufficient for Person A but not for Person B. It's best not to stretch yourself beyond your limits in order to love Person B because that's when we see an imbalance take place. In some cases, that's when we see abuse as well. Love your partner in the best way and degree you can—if that's not enough, it's best you move on. There's no shame in finding someone who shows more compatibility and appreciation for you.

Manifestation Love

Manifestation Love is in play when we want to be loved for our ability and willingness to (1) prioritize having material resources (i.e., money) available in the relationship, (2) hustle business and career-wise for the sake of the relationship and family, (3) keep a healthy social network, (4) keep up with the latest technology and social trends, (5) say what needs to be said through clever and witty conversation, and (6) prioritize having fun and enjoying the spoils of life.

Some of us show love to our partners by showering them with gifts, vacations, and clothes, and providing a comfortable material life. We know that money is a necessity in our modern, capitalist society and the acquisition of money is a burden for all of us to some degree. When we take the time and effort to remove that burden from our loved ones, we show how much we love and appreciate them in our lives. When we actually derive our happiness from making things easier by providing the material necessities of life as well as material luxuries, we are practicing Manifestation Love. It's viewed as a level of sacrifice to channel one's energy and time into making money and ensuring our partners are comfortable.

It can be called a labor of love. It's also a demonstration that we value our partners—that they're worth the effort, time, and sacrifice such that they should never be uncomfortable because of a lack of material resources.

In our society, the expression of Manifestation Love is sometimes viewed as superficial or shallow; for that reason, many of us have a hard time giving or receiving our love in that way. Those seeking a partner who practices Manifestation Love are seen as "users" or gold diggers, but that's simply a popular judgment in our society. The truth is that it's just a preference. We're all wired differently in how we give and receive love, and most of us understand the importance of material resources in our lives. Most of us appreciate receiving presents as well. The kinds of presents we like may vary, but we all like to receive them on some level. For that reason, we must try to release our judgments around those who want to be loved in that way, as well as those who use this love expression in relationships.

Another aspect of Manifestation Love is prioritizing work. In other words, those who express Manifestation Love tend to be hard-working individuals who'd like to be appreciated for their efforts. They often prioritize education, learning, and gaining practical experience as a necessity and sacrifice that should be honored. Taking the time to build yourself up so that you can earn money in a competitive world should hold value in their eyes. Not only do they work hard, but they also play hard, which brings us to another aspect of Manifestation Love. These individuals want to be recognized for their intelligence and cleverness as well. They view it as a skill that can bring value to the relationship by making it easier to navigate. In their mind, these skills can be translated into problem-solving relationship challenges as well as resolving conflicts in the partnership. Because these individuals are material focused, they are usually willing to be flexible and not make a big deal out of things. Why? Because as long as everyone has what they need materially, all other challenges can easily be worked through. Their education and focus on sales, networking, and business also make them expert communicators, which means they're always willing to talk things through. How many people do we know who'd rather not spend the time to talk through challenges and concerns in the relationship all the way through to resolution? The answer is, a lot. It's a talent to be able to talk it out. It's a talent to be able to sit for hours and talk about the relationship until all sides feel comfortable. It's a talent to know what to say and when to say it so as to not make matters worse. This is the added dimension that Manifestation Lovers bring to the table. It's not just about the money, but also the inherent skills that come with being money focused, including communication. This means seeing assets and resources as a larger goal for the family and not getting sidetracked by smaller issues around chores, time spent, etc. These individuals also like the concept of making life easier using technology, services, and tools that reduce the workload. Their cleverness and resourcefulness offer shortcuts to make things easier. You could call these timesavers "life hacks" that reduce the amount of energy we need to expend to get things done.

Those who practice Manifestation Love tend to be masculine-submissive in nature; therefore, it's their natural proclivity to work on behalf of their partners and for the relationship. We also need to realize and acknowledge the submissive aspect at play here, as all submissives want to work for the dominant person they serve. In other words, there's happiness that comes from the simple act of serving. The masculine aspect simply means they will take the initiative to make it happen and won't necessarily need direction to do it.

Not only is the ability to hustle and make money valuable in obtaining resources, but it's also a rare skill. Part of their love offering is teaching and transferring these skills onto their partners. Essentially, they are giving their partners a money mindset and teaching them how to manipulate the markets and capitalist system in order to survive. From this standpoint, they are being unselfish in their love by teaching their partners how to survive without them. This is critical, especially when we think about the possibility of them not being there in the future due to divorce, death, debilitation, or other unforeseeable circumstances. It's almost like a life insurance policy where you're practically guaranteeing your partner will be fine if you're no longer around to support them. Manifestation Lovers recognize this because they fully understand such information is hard to come by and takes practice and trial and error to cultivate.

Their love offering is also about acknowledgment, which is why Manifestation Lovers keep social networks and attend social functions with their partners. It's one thing to have material wealth, but it's another thing entirely to be seen with all your creature comforts. These individuals understand that being witnessed and acknowledged is a great way to keep the relationship on track and ensure their partners feel good about themselves. They also understand the importance of being around others who value material wealth and resources to avoid jealousy and 'hateration'. Thus, a strong social network will always be an offering Manifestation Lovers give to their partners.

Manifestation Lovers tend to be service-oriented when it comes to sex as well. They are willing to bring value in the form of sexual pleasure to their partners. This falls in line with their desire to keep things fun, light, and interesting in the relationship. They fully expect the relationship to be climactic as a result of their material bounty, but are also willing to put in the work necessary to make the sex orgasmic and pleasing on both sides. It doesn't mean they'll always succeed, but they'll try hard either way. Because they're into the material world, they're open to using gadgets to enhance their sexual experience and will often prefer to use them to spice things up. They do, however, believe in reciprocity when it comes to sex. If they put effort into bringing you pleasure, they expect the same in return. Reciprocity is big for them in all areas, not just sexually.

Lastly, Manifestation Lovers are firmly into fun and enjoyment. They believe in bringing good times to their partners as a show of their love and appreciation. We mentioned earlier they are great at sorting through relationship challenges because they are so lighthearted about things that don't impact their money. This same lightheartedness allows them to be fun-loving, funny, and into having a good time. They see this as extremely valuable, especially in a world full of stress, anxiety, and assholes. It feels good to be with someone who likes to have a good time and keeps things light. Manifestation Lovers are often comedians and are always joking around. They are willing to be the life of the party and the center of attention if need be. This makes them easy to be around and lovable in their own way.

Manifestation Lovers tend to be masculine-submissive like the NEGOTIATOR, expecting to initiate sex, anticipate their partner's needs, and be the catalyst of activity in the relationship. That said, they are perfectly fine being directed on what to do and how to go about doing it by feminine-dominant types like the LOVER. In addition, they want their partners to come to them for financial and verbal support whenever they need it. Again, they see themselves as the financial rock in their partner's life and want to be leveraged to ensure they're taken care of.

FEMININE CHOICE PARADIGM: Later on, we'll talk about the Feminine Choice Paradigm, which describes how and why the feminine and submissive elements choose partners in a relationship. In the Feminine Choice Paradigm, when a feminine or submissive person chooses to be the recipient of Manifestation Love, it's called a Manifestation Choice. In other words, they are choosing this person because of the way they love (i.e., prioritization of material resources, wealth, great communication, and the importance of specialness in the relationship) and how that love ultimately makes them feel: valuable.

Do you practice Manifestation Love? If you answer YES to most of these questions, you might express your love in this way and have NEGOTIATOR tendencies when it comes to relationships.

1. Do you see your financial status and stability as a critical prerequisite for entering a serious relationship?
2. Do you agree with Big Daddy Kane's premise: "Romance without finance, is a damn nuisance?"
3. Do you believe relationships should be fun and lighthearted?
4. Do you believe presents, money, and material offerings are a legitimate show of your love to someone?
5. Do you believe intelligence is a critical component to relationship success?
6. Do you believe financial stability is an attractive trait for someone to have?

7. Do you believe keeping up with technology is a way to keep the relationship fresh and functional?
8. Do you believe consistent, clear communication is a critical component of relationship success?

Freedom Love

Freedom Love is in play when we want to be loved for our ability and willingness to (1) bring ingenuity and creativity into the relationship; (2) know how to get things done; (3) remain open to new experiences, including sexually; (4) promote that each person be free and express themselves in a way that's comfortable for them (i.e., unconditional love); (5) stay spiritually focused; (6) multiply our position financially and otherwise; and (7) push beyond our limits and comfort zone.

Some of us see ourselves as creative geniuses and the type of people who can really improve any aspect of our lives. This is often the attitude of Freedom Lovers, who see their ingenuity as a real asset to their partners and the relationship as a whole. Freedom Lovers believe they offer gifts in the form of great insights, intelligence, and amazing perspectives, and expect to be loved and recognized for these gifts. They can be sensitive about this because these insights can be seen as intangible and sometimes hard to recognize, so their partners will really have to be in tune with them and always be willing to listen.

In line with their brilliance is their ability to understand how to get things done and move past present predicaments in order to get to the next level. Freedom Lovers have the skill of getting people "unstuck" and moving them forward to achieve success. They are able to develop a strategy and clear insights on a path forward. Yes, this is a natural talent, but it's also an expression of their love because most of their insights are taken for granted; thus, they expect recognition and appreciation for the strategies they offer their partners.

Let's get some perspective on wanting to be loved for being insightful. We currently live in the information age where information is at our fingertips, but to be honest, we're inundated with information to the point where we can't discern what's real and effective. This leaves us back where we've always been, which is: the right information is still of immense value. When we look at the fact that Fortune 500 companies spend millions of dollars per year on consultants and knowledge experts, we can start to see where executives place their trust. We see these same companies pouring millions into research and development and think tanks to figure out what to do and how to do it. Knowledge is power. Effective strategies save time and money. If you're in a crowd of people and everyone starts running in a particular direction, in most cases you'll start running in that same direction as well. Even if you don't hear or see anything, you'll still assume they know something you don't and respond in kind. This is why insider trading is illegal; when people know more than others, they can exploit the market. The point is that Freedom Lovers firmly understand the principles of useful information, strategic insights, and understanding. Many families struggle financially because they don't have the information they need to make gains. It's not that they don't have the ability or desire, but rather their efforts are being wasted due to inefficiency. The Freedom Lover represents efficiency. They are creative and can look at the world in unique ways. Offering that gift to their partners is no different than buying them a car or house in their minds. They are giving you a path to achievement as a show of their love and respect.

They also push for new experiences, which will ultimately broaden their partner's perspective and expand their intelligence. Freedom Lovers believe in growth and expansion by challenging the status quo. They see it as a necessary part of relationships and a primary way to prevent stagnation. This isn't something others will necessarily appreciate, but it is something we can all agree is a benefit. Growth is hard sometimes because it requires us to move beyond our comfort zone. Freedom Lovers are willing to go beyond boundaries and limits to achieve growth, including in the sexual arena. They are willing to try new things and make improvements to their sexual skill set while having a desire for constant improvement. This will keep their sex life from being stagnant, which will help sustain the relationship as well.

One of the biggest love expressions for Freedom Lovers is their ability to love unconditionally. The ability to allow others to be themselves or find themselves is a unique way of expressing love to others that sometimes gets lost in the modern relationship dynamic because many of us are scared of change. The Freedom Lover promotes change and expansion and is willing to still love their partner once they've made significant changes to themselves. Again, this is a unique ability, especially in a world where the statement, "You've changed" is so common as a reason for a breakup.

Those with a Freedom Love expression also tend to view themselves as bringing spiritual insights to their partners. They see their views on the esoteric and spiritual world as something valuable and delight in sharing these views with their partners. For them, offering spiritual guidance is a part of their gift to humanity, especially those they're in a relationship with.

Let's get back to the sexuality of Freedom Lovers. They might be more drawn to uncongenial relationship structures like open relating, polyamory, polygyny, polyandry, consensual non-monogamy, etc. I'm not saying they definitely desire something alternative, but they often do. They want to be loved for bringing these unconventional structures to their partner as a part of their growth and expansion. Because they are attracted to freedom in general, this may also translate to their desired relationship structures. Again, they see this as a benefit they bring to the relationship. The fact that they may be open to a threesome or swinging or to try toys or take classes on improving their sexuality is a plus, especially when they compare themselves to others who are more prude with their sexual expression. The point is they are open to trying new things and going outside of the box to make it happen. This keeps things interesting and spicy, which can help make things last. It also makes them stand out in their attractiveness. They present themselves as a free woman or man and actually dress the part. They might even look exotic, which in their mind not only honors their free expression but also adds to their uniqueness, clearly setting them apart from their peers.

When we look at all these aspects of someone who practices Freedom Love, we get another bonus aspect as well—good luck. Freedom Lovers tend to be good luck charms; the way in which they love makes you feel lucky. It makes you feel like anything is possible. It gives you hope and optimism for the future because they help us understand that rules, boundaries, and limitations are actually illusions; thus, all things are possible if we believe in them. This is a major factor in why people are attracted to this love style. At some point in our lives, it becomes necessary to believe we are limited by our education, environment, upbringing, physical or mental capabilities, glass ceilings, the economy, our looks, or anything else. Freedom Lovers instill this mindset into their partners, adding to their value in relationships.

Freedom Lovers are androgynous-dominant like the VISIONARY.

MASCULINE DESIRE PARADIGM: When a masculine or dominant person chooses back someone who Crown Chooses them, it's called fulfilling a Freedom Desire in the Masculine Desire Paradigm. In other words, they are choosing back this person because of the way their love (i.e., ability to believe in them and provide strategic direction) ultimately makes them feel—light and free.

Are you a Freedom Lover? If you answer YES to most of these questions, you might express your love in this way and have VISIONARY tendencies when it comes to relationships.

1. Do you believe someone allowing you to express yourself in the way you see fit is a show of love and support?
2. Do you believe someone loving you through your inconsistencies is a sign of their love and acceptance of you?
3. Do you believe someone supporting you in your growth is a sign of their love for you?
4. Is someone's commitment to implementing your ideas a critical requirement for you to feel loved by them?
5. Is it important that your partner accepts you for who you are even when others think you're weird or irresponsible?
6. Do you believe there's supreme value in sexual ceremony and learning new sexual techniques and methods?

Support Love

Support Love is in play when we want to be loved for our abilities and willingness to (1) stay physically present with our partner; (2) provide emotional support and comfort; (3) be the primary person responsible for the relationship; (4) be the clear head and leader of the relationship; (5) be willing to show up as a reliable representative of the relationship to family, friends, and associates; and (6) commit long term.

It's not easy to find someone to walk this long earth journey with, let alone be willing to do battle during the hard times, pick us up, and love us through the tough times. It's not always easy to find someone willing to provide the emotional support we all need as human beings. That's why Support Lovers see themselves as providing real value in relationships and desire to be loved and respected for it. These individuals show their love to others by offering their time, physical presence, and emotional support to those they care about. Their willingness to be there through the ups and the downs makes their love unique and special. Their presence also induces patience as they ride the waves of emotions and trials within the relationship. For example, having someone there to take care of you when you're sick or debilitated is a huge benefit. That's Support Love. Birthdays, holidays, anniversaries, family reunions, weddings, funerals, children, graduations, pregnancies, financial trials, court—through sickness and health they're present, steady, and without hesitation. They may or may not be great with gifts but will be solid when it comes to time.

Emotional support is often underrated in terms of its importance in our lives. We all need someone to talk to and lean on at times to help get us through. We all need someone who can empathize with our situation and offer words of encouragement. It's not even about getting sound advice (that's the role of the Freedom Lover), but rather having someone be an ear that shows they care. Support Lovers express their love in this way, investing their time into your emotional wellness. Part of this is due to the fact that they are spending each day with you and begin to learn your triggers and how to support you. The other side is that their quality of life is easier to maintain when everyone in the house is feeling great and in good spirits. A true leader understands that we're all connected and that a chain is only as strong as its weakest link. In other words, if one person is having a hard time, we'll all be having a hard time soon enough. This is not only emotional support, but also accountability in action.

Speaking of accountability, Support Lovers realize the importance of removing the emotional burden of their partner for the overall operation of the relationship. Look at this as proactive emotional support. Who's going to speak on behalf of the couple? Who's going to deal with challenges as they arise without focusing on fault or blame? Who's going to make sure things are resolved and not let problems linger and drag on forever? Who's going to take pride in the health and vitality of the relationship? Who's going to lead? This is a big deal in long-term committed relationships because of the sheer number of things that come up over time. Serious relationships don't survive when partners worry about petty things like who is to blame or who's at fault. Anyone with a mature outlook on relationships understands that casting blame doesn't resolve anything, and that the most important thing is being solution-oriented and cleaning things up as soon as possible to get things back on track. Support Lovers are willing to take on the burden to be accountable and proactive. It's their way of saying they love you and that you're an important part of their life, especially in a culture where casting blame and playing the victim is so commonplace.

Accountability is related to Support Lovers, as they generally want to be recognized as the clear head and leader in the relationship. They interpret this acknowledgment as a show of love and respect in the same way taking responsibility for the relationship is a clear expression of love to their partners.

It takes effort to be presentable to family and friends, let alone showing up to work each day. We need to be on our best behavior, dress the part, say and do the appropriate things, and smile through it all. How important is it that you'll be able to present your spouse to your family and friends, who are usually steeped in heavy judgment for a variety of reasons? The more solid your partner is, the fewer questions you'll have to answer and the smoother the holidays will go. Instead of side-eye looks, you'll receive compliments. Instead of "Are you sure?" you'll get "Nice choice." It's valuable to save your partner the stress and anxiety of facing family, friends, and coworkers by showing up as an intelligent, solid, common sense, neat, and well-presented partner. That's Support Love. Being someone you can take home to mother and father. Support Love is about being the person who answers questions about intentions, plans for the future, background, education, outlook, political affiliation, religious beliefs, etc.

When it comes to plans, isn't it comforting knowing your partner is interested and willing to be in a long-term, committed relationship with you? Doesn't that take the anxiety down a bit to know they share that value system and aren't just about playing games? The answer is yes. Being a mature adult with clear goals and focus and the ability to state what they want is also a show of love to the Support Lover.

How about sex? Support Lovers tend to be masculine-dominant individuals like the LEADER and are here to serve. They are amazing for intimacy and being tender and present during love-making. Again, they will be more connected from an emotional standpoint than most others. That being said, they may lack passion in other areas of lovemaking. Your attraction to them may be more tame than overly passionate, and that's perfectly fine. Allow them to show up for you in an intimate way while you also support them in their sexual and intimate needs so they can continue to show up how they need to in the relationship and all should be well.

Because Support Lovers are masculine-dominants like the LEADER, they expect to initiate sex, anticipate their partner's needs, and be the catalyst of activity in the relationship. However, they are perfectly fine with being directed on what to do and how to go about doing it, as long as it's not excessive. Also, they want their partners to come to them for emotional support whenever they need it. Again, they see themselves as the rock in their partner's life and want to be leveraged to ensure that's reinforced.

FEMININE CHOICE PARADIGM: When a feminine or submissive person chooses to be the recipient of Support Love, it's called a Support Choice in the Feminine Choice Paradigm. In other words, they're choosing this person because of how their love (i.e., prioritization of emotional support, protection, and physical presence in the relationship) ultimately makes them feel— supported, protected, and covered.

Are you a Support Lover? If you answer YES to most of these questions, you might express your love in this way and have LEADER tendencies when it comes to relationships.

1. Do you feel that simply being physically present with someone is a show of love?

2. Do you feel that taking care of all the basics of living is a show of love?
3. Do you feel that taking responsibility for the household and relationship is a show of love?
4. Do you feel that taking responsibility off your partner (I.e., financial, work, and social) is a show of love?
5. Is it important that you are honored as the head of the relationship and family in how your partner treats you and in how they present you to others?
6. Do you feel it's important to support your partner emotionally?
7. Do you believe it's important to indicate your long-term commitment to the relationship?

Soul Love

Soul Love is in play when we want to be loved for our ability and willingness to (1) focus on a mission that goes beyond our individual goals, and (2) prioritize our spiritual growth and development as a critical component of the relationship.

Some of us love because of a higher purpose and mission that we're on with our partners. We see the mission as the center of the union, as opposed to the individual needs of each person. Yes, we get our needs met, but the deal breaker is when one of us betrays the mission. When that happens, the relationship is over because it never was about you or I but rather something higher. The ultimate ability to deny ourselves in the pursuit of something bigger is the Soul Love expression here. The term "soul" refers to that which is intangible and beyond physical gratification. We are Soul Lovers when we connect with our partners through the mission.

Inherent in Soul Love is our ability to support one another in our spiritual growth and development (however we define it). Soul

Love is about loving our partners because of their efforts to elevate themselves while accomplishing the mission at hand. It's loving the effort and struggle of detachment from sensual gratification and everything that feeds the standard relationship (i.e., romance, finance, family, sexuality, Passion, acknowledgment, etc.) and moving into something higher, something beyond. It's nurturing the feeling and belief that we've been here before and that we were destined to meet to do this work. This is Soul Love.

This doesn't mean that standard needs aren't met or prioritized in the relationship; it simply means that they are not a top priority. In other words, they will never be deal breakers in the relationship, but rather things to be transcended on their path to doing the larger work of the mission.

Soul Love occurs when the focus is on elevating one's highest personal and spiritual heights while also reconnecting with source energy (i.e., their creator, whether science, spiritual, or religious-based). It's the recognition that we are beyond our personality, material ownership, and accomplishments and simply honor the reflection of ourselves we see in the other person. When someone says, "I see the god/goddess in you," they demonstrate their love by how they treat you and react to your many behaviors. Their love is not conditional or based on what they can do for you, but rather the simple fact of their existence and you getting to see them fully.

The elevation of one's awareness and natal indwelling consciousness activates Soul Love. However, the minute personal and spiritual elevation no longer become a priority, the love falters. Soul Lovers also prioritize the mission over their partners, meaning if their partners lose interest in the mission (whatever it may be), their love may diminish. Soul Lovers consider abandoning the common mission as violation of the partnership.

Soul Lovers tend to be androgynous-neutral types like the PEACEKEEPER. Their androgynous nature causes them to flow as their environment dictates; however, they can be independent and do not necessarily have to engage with others. This is a case where they prefer their mission over connection.

FEMININE CHOICE PARADIGM: When a feminine or submissive person chooses to be the recipient of Soul Love, it's called a Soul Choice in the Feminine Choice Paradigm. In other words, they're choosing this person because of how their love (i.e., prioritization of a common mission over one's welfare) ultimately makes them feel—philanthropic, giving, and beyond worldly influences.

MASCULINE DESIRE PARADIGM: When a masculine or dominant person chooses someone who Soul Chooses them, it's called a fulfilling of Soul Desire in the Masculine Desire Paradigm. In other words, they are choosing back this person because of the way their love (i.e., prioritization of a common mission over one's welfare, as well as a desire for things to be balanced in their environment) ultimately makes them feel—philanthropic, giving, and beyond worldly influence.

NOTE: Soul Love is the only expression that is aligned to both Feminine Choice and Masculine Desire. All other love expressions are aligned with one or the other.

If you express your love in this way, you'd be considered as a Soul Lover. Frequently, those who love others in this way desire or choose other Soul Lovers in their lives.

Are you a Soul Lover? If you answer YES to most of these

questions, you might express your love in this way and have PEACEKEEPER tendencies when it comes to relationships.

1. Do you love your partner for their commitment to a higher purpose?
2. Do you love your partner regardless of how they treat you as long as they follow the mutually agreed upon mission?
3. Do you love your partner regardless of how things are going financially, communication-wise, sexually, etc.?
4. Is it hard for you to love someone who doesn't have a higher mission and gets caught up in the material world?
5. Is it important that your partner is able to let go of their attachments to things, people, philosophies, circumstances, etc. on behalf of personal growth?
6. Is your partner not working on their spiritual growth and development a deal breaker for you?

Devoted Love

Devoted Love is in play when we want to be loved for our ability and willingness to (1) stay committed to our partner and the relationship; (2) stay devoted to our partner's dreams and goals; (3) take care of the responsibilities within the relationship and family regardless of the health of the relationship; (4) provide a quiet presence; (5) be a trusted confidant; (6) represent the family with nobility and class; and (7) nurture our partner, the children, and the relationship as a whole.

Some show their love through a willingness and ability to commit to their partners. Commitment is the ability to be mentally locked in and bonded to your partner without the need for specific outside influences or circumstances. This means it doesn't take cars, money, a particular type of house, etc. to stay committed in the relationship. This is Devoted Love, where we are mentally and emotionally bonded with our partners and do not allow external circumstances to influence the idea we have about what the partnership is. We're not talking about faith, which involves hope and knowing things will become what we want; instead, it's the ability to live inside of the reality we have chosen. In other words, the marriage is what we are envisioning right now, rather than tomorrow or the future. Commitment is about staying present with the vision. This is a skill that eludes most people. When we see how hard it is to remain committed to our diet, our exercise routines, or our budgets, it becomes clear just how valuable this is in relationships. Devoted Lovers offer commitment as a show of their love and support to their partners and families. For these individuals, it's the highest offering they can make.

Staying with the theme of commitment, Devoted Lovers also believe in their partner's hopes, dreams, and goals. There is complete buy-in for who they can be and their ability to achieve greatness, and they treat their partner as if they have already achieved success in the here and now. We all know how good it feels when someone truly believes in us and wants nothing but the absolute best for us in all our endeavors. It feels like love, and it feels amazing to our hearts and spirit. Not only does it feel amazing, but it's also helpful in terms of actualizing our goals. It gives us an extra push and belief to keep going and know that we'll be successful. This is how Devoted Lovers show their love to their partners.

Another aspect of Devoted Love is the dedication to duties and responsibilities of family and relationships regardless of the ups and downs. Devoted Lovers never leverage their responsibilities in order to get their way in a relationship. Instead, they do what needs to be done even during times of strife and choose a different approach to working things out. They won't quit on their partners and never stop believing in them and their dreams just because the relationship is experiencing difficulties. This is the ultimate show of love and reverence for their partner. Another way to say it is that they'll never go on strike due to conflict.

Devoted Lovers also show their love by being quietly observant. For them, bringing about peace and tranquility in their environment will further harmonize their relationship and help energize their partner by minimizing stress. Creating a quiet, peaceful, and clean environment isn't always an easy thing to do, especially when children are involved. For Devoted Lovers, this is a labor of love for their partners.

The other side of remaining quiet is being a confidant for their partners and someone they can show their emotions to. A Devoted Lover is someone who their partners can cry with or freely express any emotion; maintaining that sharing in confidence is critical to creating intimacy in the relationship. They are also someone their partner can trust to share their deepest thoughts, feelings, and dreams with, which is a trait they value as well. In their minds, having someone to share absolutely anything with and knowing it will be done in complete confidence is one of the highest forms of love and respect that partners can bring to any relationship.

There's something to be said when someone is mindful about representing you in the highest regard to family, friends, and associates. This can be done through their appearance, what they say and how they say it, and through their attitude. Some people don't value consistently representing themselves and their partner in the highest light, which makes this love expression even more valuable. Again, it feels good knowing your partner will always have your back when interacting with others. It feels good knowing they will always present themselves in the very best way they can. It also feels good knowing they won't betray your trust and confidence. This is Devoted Love.

Much of what has been described involves the Devoted Lover's ability to nurture their partner, to build them up when they're low, and to make them whole again. Devoted Love is critical when children are involved. Still, it is valued by those who need to be put back together because of the amount of energy they sacrifice for work or otherwise. This is a very specific and intentional expression of love that takes time and focus. Pouring your heart into someone and giving your time and energy to nurse others back into strength isn't something that comes easy for everyone. Also, not everyone is willing to put in that kind of effort for their partners—or anyone else, for that matter.

We mentioned earlier that Devoted Love is about the consistent execution of one's duty inside of the relationship. This translates into sex as well, where going to bed angry and withholding sex is never an option. For the Devoted Lover, maintaining a healthy sexual connection with their partner is critical for sustaining intimacy and trust in the relationship. Since they regard sexual interaction as healing for the partnership, they always make sure to show up sexually for their partner. They are also willing to do a variety of things sexually and will be completely open and receptive to what their partners need and desire.

Devoted Lovers tend to be feminine-submissive archetypes like the DEVOTEE. Their feminine energy allows them to be committed to their partners and family, while their submissive roles make them excellent at following leaders. Masculine-dominant archetypes like the LEADER will often best compliment them.

MASCULINE DESIRE PARADIGM: When a masculine or dominant person chooses back someone who Supports Chooses them, it's called a fulfilling of Devoted Desire. In other words, they are choosing back this person because of the way their love (i.e., ability to nurture and take care of them, believe in them, work on behalf of the relationship) makes them feel.

Are you a Devoted Lover? If you answer YES to most of these questions, you might express your love in this way and have DEVOTEE tendencies when it comes to relationships.

1. Do you believe dedication to performing your duties in the relationship is critical to maintaining a healthy, committed relationship?
2. Do you believe nurturing and taking care of the family and your partner is a critical function of love?
3. Do you believe you should be number one in your partner's life based on the fact that you put in the work for the relationship to justify it?
4. Do you believe it's important to set a proper impression for those outside of your relationship?
5. Is it important to maintain your role in the relationship regardless of how you and your partner are getting along at the time?
6. Do you believe being committed to your partner's dreams and goals is a critical component of relationship success?
7. Do you believe commitment to your partner should be independent of finances, social status, sex life, or level of happiness in the relationship at any particular time?

Crown Love

Crown Love is in play when we want to be loved for our ability and willingness to (1) set goals for ourselves, our partner, and the relationship; (2) keep our partner informed of the deeper meaning of the phenomena in their lives; (3) stay true to morals and help instill those morals within the relationship; (4) guide our partner in finding their life purpose; and (5) show a willingness to be purpose-driven while supporting our partner in doing the same.

One way to express our love is by establishing and adhering to principles that we are to live by as a couple and family. Some would argue that without a philosophical guide to life (whether religious or otherwise), there is simply no way to achieve success and happiness. There must be a measure and series of guides to keep us on course, and the relationship needs someone to be the keeper of these principles. Keepers of the principles ensure everyone is on track and in alignment so that the relationship can stay in integrity and be about something more than just sex, bills, and survival. Crown Lovers maintain the integrity of the relationship so that everyone is clear on what's expected and how things are moving forward. This could include philosophies around God and spirituality, diet, relationship structures, raising children, and how the family fits into the local political structure. These philosophies themselves, the corresponding protocols that everyone follows, as well as the willingness to be the keeper and overseer of them are seen as valuable expressions of the love these individuals have for their partners.

These principles are two-fold: (1) they're there to help the relationship; and (2) they're there to support individual growth. Crown Lovers are similar to Freedom Lovers in that they believe in growth and expansion of the individual; however, their methods are different. Crown Lovers believe the system itself along with its series of protocols is the path to expansion, whereas Freedom Lovers believe it's about organic experiences. Either way, Crown Lovers are certainly interested in your growth—not just spiritually, but also in becoming a better you and developing your character. It may seem scary to the average person to invest in the relationship in this way, particularly out of fear of losing their partner once they reach a certain level of development. It takes a special person to have faith in the process and a belief that they will be loved for offering this kind of support to their partner.

As mentioned before, we are in the information age; however, quality information still comes at a premium. Crown Lovers offer special insight into the reality of the world and they only share this offering with those who appreciate their perspective. If a person sees something for what it is such that it could save others time, money, and even heartache, most people would want that information. However, there must be a reason to give it. Crown Lovers share this perspective with their partners because they love and want the best for them. They also want their partners to experience success and avoid heartache whenever possible.

Another aspect of sharing information is about guidance. Because Crown Lovers are naturally masculine-dominant, they take it upon themselves to provide guidance wherever possible to those around them. In many cases, they truly have a mastery over a particular skill or area of life, and their desire to share that experience for the sake of improving the lives of their partners is a key love expression.

Crown Lovers are not just about believing in your dreams, but also about helping you craft them. It's one thing to have someone who believes in a goal you've already determined on your own, but what about those of us who need help finding our purpose and creating goals? What about those of us who haven't found ourselves and are searching for our passion and the truth of who we are? That's the offering of the Crown Lover, where clarity and conviction about your life is their passion. This obviously helps the relationship as well because it's much easier to relate to someone who's clear on their purpose than to someone who is unsure and lost. Crown Lovers are about bringing this clarity to their loved ones.

Crown Lovers tend to be androgynous-submissive archetypes like the MONK. Due to their androgynous nature, they tend to flow wherever their environment takes them, while their submissive nature puts them into a service position wherever they go. They are often complimented best by androgynous-dominant archetypes like the VISIONARY.

FEMININE CHOICE PARADIGM: When a feminine or submissive person chooses to be the recipient of Crown Love, it's called a Crown Choice. In other words, they are choosing this person because of the way they love (i.e., the ability to provide deep mental and spiritual healing and satisfaction as well as guiding their lives).

Are you a Crown Lover? If you answer YES to most of these questions, you might express your love in this way and have MONK tendencies when it comes to relationships.

1. Do you believe it's important to follow specific protocols in a relationship for the relationship to work?
2. Do you believe individual and relationship goals are important for a relationship to survive?

3. Is it important that your partner recognizes your insights and intelligence by implementing what you say?
4. Is it important that you and your partner engage in deep conversation around the meaning and direction of the relationship?
5. Do you believe that relationships operate best when they follow a clear philosophy?
6. Do you believe that helping them understand their purpose in the world is a fundamental way to guide your partner?

Romantic Love

Romantic Love is in play when we want to be loved for our ability and willingness to (1) maintain one's beauty and appearance to ensure positive feng shui (i.e., environment) and a high value relationship, (2) present ourselves well to make our partner's brand and value go up, (3) prioritize the specialness of the relationship (anniversaries, holidays, birthdays, special events, trips, etc.), (4) bring sweetness to our partner without any conflict, and (5) fulfill our partner's sexual desires to the best of our ability.

We know the importance of a beautiful environment because of its ability to lift our spirits and mood. Well, people are a part of that environment as well, and how we present ourselves can have the same effect as new construction; art pieces; a clean, fresh, nicely decorated room; or colorful flowers to light up a dining room. We know that people are willing to pay for beautiful things and to be in stunningly beautiful surroundings. Why? Because it makes us feel great. Sometimes, our gift to our loved ones is to be a beautiful and vibrant part of the environment. This means always looking amazing so we can feel amazing about ourselves and our choice in a partner. Beauty involves work, and some are willing to sacrifice their time and energy to appear beautiful, appealing, and attractive to the eye. Beauty is also a part of the fantasy of romance—not only is the love connection there, but also the outward appearance of the connection between two people. It's the same way that we envision a wedding where the colors, flowers, music, cake, and presentation of bridesmaids and groomsmen all come together in a crescendo of beauty.

Another part of being tied to beauty is that it helps your value go up due to its scarcity in the world. There's a reason models get paid so much to sell products and services for major corporations. Most beautiful people know that when they are with their partners, their partner's value increases. Doors that were once closed suddenly open. People who didn't want to be around you are suddenly interested in spending time or talking with you. This is the power of beauty and grace. It's a gift for beautiful people to intentionally represent themselves in a way that supports their partners in increasing their value among their peers. This is part of the Romantic Love expression.

Romantic relationships are about specialness, meaning there must be something about the relationship that makes it stand out from other relationships. Each person in the relationship must be made to feel special—it's all part of the presentation of romance. For someone to support you in feeling special by presenting themselves in a way that sets them apart from other people is special indeed. Supporting someone in feeling special isn't easy, but the offering is the love expression of the Romantic Lover.

Romantic Lovers also refuse to bring drama into their relationships. Their predominant presentation is one of sweetness, amenability, submission, and support. They show their love through being easy to get along with and avoiding justifications for conflict.

They love others by being flexible and willing to go with the flow. As long as they feel loved, they won't make anything a big deal. They fully understand most people are full of drama when it comes to certain aspects of relating, so they pride themselves on avoiding drama whenever they can. They pride themselves on being the person you'd most like to be around because of their sweetness.

Sweetness is also something Romantic Lovers bring to the bedroom. They are always willing to be precisely what their partners desire them to be. It's a part of their submission to be soft, amenable, and willing to please their partner in a variety of ways. For Romantic Lovers, this is an important way to demonstrate love to their partner—by being open to their sexual needs and desires.

They make you feel like the burdens of life are an illusion; their love elevates you to new heights of happiness above what you experience on a day-to-day basis. Their goal and gift is to remind you that no matter how you're feeling, there's always something beautiful waiting for you at home.

Romantic lovers tend to be feminine-dominant archetypes like the LOVER. Their best reciprocators are masculine-submissive archetypes like the NEGOTIATOR.

MASCULINE DESIRE PARADIGM: When a masculine or dominant person chooses back someone who Romantic Chooses them, it's called a fulfilling of Love Desire. In other words, they are choosing back this person because of the way their love (i.e., make your brand go up and be a part of a beautiful environment and space) makes them feel.

Are you a Romantic Lover? If you answer YES to most of these questions, you might express your love in this way and have LOVER tendencies when it comes to relationships.

1. Are special days (i.e., Valentine's Day, anniversaries, etc.) critical to celebrate for a relationship to survive?
2. Are public appearances with your partner important in keeping the relationship fresh and viable?
3. Is public acknowledgment of your specialness critical for you to feel love from your partner?
4. Is a partner who prioritizes and supports you in keeping your looks, beauty, and upkeep an important factor in feeling they love you?
5. Is your partner giving you beautiful things (i.e., clothes, jewelry, vacations, etc.) a prerequisite to feeling they love you?
6. Are compliments about your looks, style, and personal expressions important to you in feeling love from your partner?
7. Do you believe that being low-drama is an asset to the relationship?
8. Do you believe that being open and receptive to what your partner desires sexually is important to maintaining a healthy relationship?

Womb Love

Womb Love is in play when we want to be loved for our ability and willingness to (1) satisfy our partner's deepest sexual needs, (2) make personal sacrifices on behalf of our partner (i.e., security, protection, etc.), and (3) work hard on behalf of the relationship to ensure it has everything that's needed (i.e., working a job or doing chores).

Some people naturally hold the key to unlock our physical pleasures more so than others. There are many reasons for this, but regardless, it appears to be true in many cases. Some are willing to give their physical body far more intensely than others. Giving of the body is of no lesser value than giving of the heart, soul, or mind. It's really about what our partners prioritize as valuable in their lives and why. Often, sexual healing ranks high on the list of physical offerings. The gift of offering your body to bring your partner to the heights of pleasure is rare indeed; although many people may have that intention, not everyone has cultivated their body to be consistently effective in that way. Physical, sexual skills are like beauty—they are cultivated and developed. Investing the time and energy to be a vessel of sexual pleasure should be honored like any other cultivated skill. The Womb Lover offers their physical essence to their partner as a show of love and dedication. They know that physical pleasure and sexual release are valuable experiences, and that most people don't have access to high-quality sexual interaction with their partner. This is their gift. It's their show of love. When we look at the number of people who experience true health benefits from high-quality sexual intercourse, we can see the value. Whether it's the elimination of or reduction in stress and anxiety, improved menstrual cycles, or a simple elevation of mood, the value is clear. No drugs are required—just human touch and connection.

Womb Lovers offer their partners good love as an expression of their appreciation. It's usually not just quality, but quantity as well. They are willing to make love frequently with the same intensity and passion, which takes care of all of their partner's sexual needs.

However, the physical sacrifices and offerings go beyond sex, of course. These individuals are willing to work hard for their partners when it comes to making money, doing chores, being protective over the house, and doing whatever work needs to be done.

Womb Love is described as showing love in a physical, visceral, and sexually passionate way. It occurs when someone displays a consistent work ethic and an ability to sacrifice their physical comfort on behalf of their partners and the family. These individuals tend to be hard workers and see their work as a labor of love for their partners. Womb Love stands separate from other forms of love in its consistent ability to connect partners in a visceral way sexually. This sexual interaction tends to be very orgasmic and beyond what we would be able to experience with the average lover. It's about tapping into the needs of the physical body such that it's honored and stretched to its maximum capacity to feel.

For example, my wife and I are in an open marriage, and she has a Womb Choice but expresses her love back to him through Devoted Love. He gives her the visceral sex she desires, and she shows as a nurturer to him and his son. She initially tried to love him based on her standard expression of love—Crown Love—but it wasn't what he was looking for in exchange for being a Womb Choice.

In return, Womb Choices expect to be deeply loved and respected for their efforts. They see their ability to put their needs to the side and use their energy for things benefiting the relationship as something worthy of love. They see their ability to activate the body through sex as a specialty that should be honored by submission. This is why when a Womb Choice approaches their partner, they fully expect them to submit to their will and wishes. They have no problem initiating communication or contact. Still, once it's initiated, they'd rather not debate about what needs to be done or how to interpret what's happening with the relationship. It's not about them being right or wrong, but an expectation they have to have their needs met first.

Womb Lovers tend to be masculine-neutral archetypes like the SOLDIER and expect to initiate sex and be the catalyst of activity in the relationship. However, because they're in a neutral position, they expect their partners to anticipate their needs and provide for them without solicitation, which can be interpreted as selfishness. They also expect their partners to be responsive when they state their needs and desires. Because they are in the masculine, they expect their partners to come to them for protection, security, and to get challenging things done. Again, they see themselves as the rock in their partner's life and want to be leveraged to ensure that's the case.

FEMININE CHOICE PARADIGM: When a feminine or submissive person chooses to be the recipient of Womb Love, it's called a Womb Choice in the Feminine Choice Paradigm. In other words, they are choosing this person because of the way they love (i.e., ability to provide deep sexual healing and satisfaction as well as providing protection and security) and ultimately how that love makes them feel—physically healed.

Are you a seeker of Womb Love? If you answer YES to most of these questions, you might express your love in this way and have SOLDIER tendencies when it comes to relationships.

1. Is sexual passion between you and your partner a critical factor in your relationship thriving and surviving?
2. Does your happiness hinge on how passionate and frequent your sexual interaction is with your partner?
3. Is it important for you to sacrifice your comfort at times as an indication of your love for your partner?
4. Is it important that your partner recognizes and loves you based on the work you put in with jobs, work, chores, etc.?
5. Is it important that your partner recognizes your sacrifices on behalf of the relationship?

Summary of the Love Expressions

We need to figure out which love expression we gravitate toward the most so we can understand what we're looking for and the kinds of standards we tend to hold others to as well. This is important. It's also important to understand that everyone loves differently—it's never personal, but simply a preference or what we're used to. The love expression is the key to understanding where we are in our GE-PR Matrix, as either a masculine-dominant, masculine-submissive, feminine-dominant, or feminine-submissive type of person. Identifying this designation will help us understand our role in our partner's lives as well as their role in ours. For example, we'll never look to a feminine-submissive partner to initiate sex consistently or to initiate a much-needed talk in the relationship. We'll look to the masculine-submissive or masculine-dominant to do that. Conversely, we'll better understand why our masculine-dominant partner has a hard time coming out of their ego if they're used to setting the tone for everything or if they feel the world should cater to them because of their accomplishments, swagger, confidence, etc. We can also look at past relationships and realize why we may have bumped heads or couldn't maneuver through disconnects and arguments with any consistency. Maybe one partner was a feminine-dominant, the other was a masculine-dominant, and no one wanted to budge from their particular viewpoints. Or maybe one partner was a feminine-submissive, the other was a feminine-dominant, and neither ended up initiating conversations or taking the lead on conflict resolution exercises.

The following table lists the 9 Expressions of Love. It provides a summary description of each love expression, generally which archetype practices that expression of love, and which Feminine Choice or Masculine Desire corresponds to that specific love expression.

Love Expression Summary Table

Love Expression	Summary Description	Archetype	Feminine Choice	Masculine Desire
Power Love	–Prioritizes their partner over everyone else –Does rituals on their behalf –Creates a formal, safe container to relate in (i.e., marriage), –Maintains privacy, –Brings intense sexual interaction	CONSERVATIONIST		Power Desire
Manifestation Love	–Supplies material comforts and luxuries, –Provides fun and lightness to the relationship, –Maintains social networks of like-minded people, –Maintains excellent communication, –Doesn't get stuck on relationship drama	NEGOTIATOR	Manifestation Choice	
Freedom Love	–Brings the sex rituals, –Brings strategy to their partner for their success and their relationship success, –Willing to be adventurous and try new things, –willing to try different relationship structures, –Supports their partner in being free from the burdens of life, –Promotes learning and personal growth, –Good luck charm	VISIONARY		Freedom Desire
Support Love	–Provides consistent presence in the relationship, –Provides emotional support to their partner, –Serves as a solid representative to family, friends, and associates, –Willing to take responsibility and leadership position in the relationship, –Ensure long-term commitment to the relationship	LEADER	Support Choice	
Soul Love	–Wants to build something larger than themselves, –Willing to put their wants and desires to the side for the sake of the larger mission, –Willing to break attachments and addictions for the mission, –Passion for expressing themselves as creators in the world	PEACEKEEPER	Soul Choice	Soul Desire
Devoted Love	–Performs their responsibilities regardless of the state of the relationship, –Provides a quiet presence, –Is a trusted confidant, –Represents the family and leadership well (i.e., nobility), –Nurtures their partner and family, –Stays committed for the long-term	DEVOTEE		Devotional Desire
Crown Love	–Sets goals for their partner, relationship, and family, –Keeps partner informed of deeper aspects of life events happening, –Creates and sticks to protocols and morals, –Willing to be purpose-driven on behalf of the relationship	MONK	Crown Choice	
Romantic Love	–Willing to maintain one's beauty and appearance to maintain positive feng shui of relationship and maintain its high value, –Presents themselves well to make partner's brand and value go up, –Prioritizes the specialness of the relationship (anniversaries, holidays, birthdays, special events, trips, etc.), –Brings sweetness to their partner without any conflict, –Fulfills partner's sexual desires	LOVER		Love Desire
Womb Love	–Satisfies their partner's deep sexual needs beyond the normal, –Makes personal sacrifices on behalf of their partner (i.e., security, protection, etc.), –Works hard on behalf of the relationship to ensure it has what's needed (i.e., working a job or doing chores, etc.)	SOLDIER	Womb Choice	

Part 3: Choice, Desire, & Relating

The Feminine Choice Paradigm™

When a woman chooses a partner, she's doing it from her feminine, submissive, or a combination of these states of being. Her feminine is saying, "This person matches the vision of a person I had in my desired relationship vision," while the submissive within her is saying, "I want to experience and grow from what this person has to teach me." Either way, she's choosing to select a particular man to facilitate her relationship experience. Overall, there are four basic needs women have that are expressed in who they choose as a partner. These needs are both practical and metaphysical, meaning women choose men to support them in a very specific way as part of their life needs while also seeking to fulfill a longing from within that can only be satisfied by their compliment.

The premise behind "choice" and attraction is a profound intelligence and wisdom. It's not a sensual, superficial thing, but rather an inner knowing of the body, mind, and soul of a woman. The Feminine Choice Paradigm (FCP) is about women learning to trust that wisdom and translate it into a relationship that properly feeds them. All attractions are not equal. All attractions aren't feeding you in the same way. We must learn to sort out what is what and who is who and act accordingly. If women can do this, they will begin to trust themselves and their feminine intuitions, leading to a happier life. The more tools at our disposal to navigate our lives, the better.

Another aspect of women being the choosers in relationships has more to do with the survival of the human species, involving their role as "gatekeeper" for which genes and human traits are manifested in future generations. This means women select ("choose") men based on an instinctual drive for producing the most physically capable and intelligent human beings. It's a biological program that's supposed to guarantee the evolution of the human species (or mutation, depending on your evolutionary beliefs) into its highest potential as a group of organisms. From this perspective, women are clearly the choosers of men, and this fact plays out in our dating rituals, where men attempt to demonstrate their sexual prowess, masculinity, dominance, and propensity for success and survival given the environmental conditions. We're not just talking about an intellectual decision, but also a biological decision. Some men make her heart race, her pussy wet, and her mind scattered. She's not intellectually willing her pussy to be wet at the sight of certain men; it simply happens because of her programming. As stated earlier, there is an intelligence that's hard for both men and women to accept because these responses often go against cultural norms and ideas of being an advanced species. We pride ourselves on being above animals, even though that's exactly what we are at our core. We not only see this in the human family but in the animal kingdom as well, where the female is the gatekeeper to reproduction. She's the chooser of the strongest males, and those are the ones she mates with. It's not the females fighting with one another to mate with the males. We see the strongest male mate with all of the females, which further illuminates the idea of feminine choice. In other words, males don't seem to care who they mate with as long as they can mate.

That being said, let's dig a little deeper into the types of choices women make so we can recognize which choice is being made and why. The FCP includes both feminine and submissive choice and can be broken down into five categories:

- Womb Choice – The need to be in the presence of physical superiority

- Crown Choice – The need to be in the presence of mental superiority
- Support Choice – The need to have someone take care of you and be responsible for aspects of your life
- Manifestation Choice – The need for material gratification, to feel special, and to feel loved
- Soul Choice – The need to align yourself with a mission and activity greater than yourself

Womb Choice

When a woman desires to submit to a man's physicality, she's Womb Choosing him. She's essentially looking for a man who carries the energy of the SOLDIER (i.e., Ogun, Warrior, and Herukhuti) archetype. This means she wants to be dominated sexually to the point where she is in total submission to him. In so doing, she unlocks her deepest orgasmic pleasure because she no longer has to think during sex. Thinking during sex is a woman's biggest obstacle to achieving her deepest levels of orgasm. Thus, finding a man she can surrender and submit to allows her to experience sex for what it's meant to be, while also achieving its healing benefits.

This is a case where she's submitting to superior masculine energy—most importantly, one she can't control. What separates the SOLDIER is his neutrality and indifference to connecting with others. He'll do it, but he isn't seeking connection, which makes him extremely attractive to those in the feminine. Even though the SOLDIER can't be controlled, the feminine will try anyway, which will only lead to frustration. What will also lead to frustration is her desire to be dominated by him. Still, the SOLDIER is not a dominant because he has no interest in guiding or being connected to others. Again, his lack of interest in taking the role of a dominant will cause frustration among women attempting to submit to him. He's able to stay neutral and disconnected because he doesn't want anything from anyone; thus, he can't be bribed or coerced. In addition, he can't be guilt-tripped into doing favors or abandoning his mission to service those who are choosing. Any attempts to do so will result in further frustration for those choosing him. The ultimate implication is that the SOLDIER can't be domesticated and brought into a family unit or structure. His appeal is that he exists outside of those structures—in the wild, so to speak. He's beyond structure, rules, governance, and socialization.

We mentioned earlier that the feminine gender energy is unable to connect expeditiously with what she encounters in the physical world; thus, she's not able to surrender very easily. Trust related to who she's with isn't always there. She's often unsure or still experiencing questions about him or his intentions. These issues prevent her from being able to choose her partner fully and limits her orgasm. However, when she meets a man matching her vision of a true warrior who can liberate her sexually and who she can trust and let go with, she Womb Chooses him. This essentially means she instantly trusts him.

Without question, this is a full need and not just a want or superficial desire for women. This isn't about procreation either, which is a different type of biological need and desire. The physical, sexual need for humans is like eating and should be considered as equally important. Failure to realize this will keep our society in the dark regarding the true nature of humanity and not allow us to support one another properly.

Also sought in this choice is the physical protection and security that comes with being in the presence of a physically dominant human who can't be tamed or told what to do. Women feel more relaxed when they are in the presence of a physically imposing man who is fully in his masculine energy. It's not just about being in the presence of any man, but rather one where they can feel his imposition. This allows her to stay relaxed and at least slightly moist as her primary state of being.

However, women can't necessarily expect these men to show up as dedicated, responsible husbands in their life. We're not saying they can't or won't, but generally they have a specific focus—to fuck you good and get their work done. They might not be able to provide you the emotional support you need. They might not want to settle down with you because they have ten other women vying for the same sexual satisfaction as you are. If he's fucking you incredibly well, chances are he's fucking others incredibly well too. It is what it is. His talents and abilities are universal in most cases. The point is that these men may not want to settle down and be husbands. They may want to play the field, or better yet, get the best deal for their talents, meaning they may wait for a woman who isn't acting crazy as fuck and who will offer financial or other support as an exchange for slanging mean penis—just saying.

Let's look at this from the crazy angle first. Most women aren't getting the kind of sex they need; when they find it, they tend to lose their minds. It's like a poor person winning the lottery. The first thing they do is buy a bunch of stuff and waste their money, instead of being a caretaker for it and appreciating what they've received. This is how a lot of women act with their Womb Choices—crazy as fuck, calling and texting every day, even crying or begging him to come over and be their man, or asking him why he's talking to other bitches. Basically, these kinds of things push him away and compel him to look for other sane women to interact with. If you act this way after meeting your Womb Choice, it indicates that you need to get more good dick in your life. It means you're living in sexual poverty and you need to get some more experience. Trust us—it's not meant for you to be with only him as the end all, be all. We know women won't want to hear this, but it's the truth. If you're crazy over your Womb Choice, you need to do better. You need to take ownership of your sexuality. You need to own your orgasm. We realize we may be talking to a wall here because one of the ways many women know they've found a Womb Choice is that they lose all rationality. The point is that you're going to spend all of your time trying to make him your husband and it won't work. Why? Because you're the one seeking him and not vice versa. You're not choosing him because he needs to make a change—you're choosing him because you need to up your sex game. You can't tell someone what to do when they don't want anything from you. You need to follow instructions and learn acceptance. You need to learn appreciation and love while accepting the gift of sexual awakening. This is what a Womb Choice is and does.

He's not interested in talking to you. He doesn't really want to hear about your day. He doesn't want to be sexually exclusive with you. None of the above applies. Does he love you? Yes, he does. He cares about you and wants the best for you, but his love won't manifest as Support Choice or husband love, which is a structured, domesticated form of love. We're not trying to destroy your hopes and dreams here; rather, we are simply explaining the difference between being in a position of want and need versus a position of indifference.

Now, let's talk about some hard truths around femininity for the ladies. If you find yourself really into your Womb Choice and acting a little crazy (i.e., trying to tie him down, over texting, stalking, trying to control him, etc.), it probably means you're in serious need of working on your femininity (i.e., magnetism). It also means you're likely being asked to cultivate your feminine energy such that you can be in a peaceful place regarding a man providing true sexual healing in your life. If you're into him like that, you're probably nowhere near that place and will have to go through the initiation of getting there. You'll have to challenge your established boundaries. You'll have to learn to follow directions. You'll have to trust the process and intelligence of your attraction. You'll have to resist the temptation of manipulating him into giving you what you want (i.e., fitting within your comfort zone). The attraction is not about your comfort zone, but rather your healing. You've attracted a man into your life that you can't stop thinking about for a reason: to heal and grow. The faster you give into the process, the quicker you'll enjoy being physically healed by his magic hands and phallus.

The Womb Choice is a hard concept for many of us to accept because we live in a conservative culture that castigates sex as a sin thanks to religion. It's viewed as evil, although necessary, for reproduction. Thus, it's an evil that must be tolerated on some level. If we don't understand the history of Western culture's attempt to control women, it might be hard to even look at the concept of a Womb Choice as being valid. The castigation and subjugation of women center on their sexuality, which has always been immensely intimidating toward men who have struggled to master their masculinity. In particular, those who we would consider beta males have always been scared of women and their sexuality; thus, they've tried to control it. Throughout history, these beta males couldn't master women's sexuality from a physical standpoint, so they attempted to do so through rules and religion. They essentially attempted to outlaw women's feminine nature such that they could only express it at a level matching their physicality as beta men. We know it sounds like a concept from the 1500s (which it is), but it's still the predominant thought in modern Western culture. The more things change, the more they stay the same. The beta male in Western culture is still scared of women's sexual nature— a nature, mind you, that was designed to ensure the survival of the human race. This leads to why the Womb Choice concept rubs so many people, both men and women alike, the wrong way. The thought among beta males is that women won't choose them because natural selection has dictated they aren't the strongest priority for reproduction. In other words, being nice, following the rules, and having a good education are not prerequisites for the future of the species—based on women (i.e., the gatekeepers that decide who survives into the future) who are Womb Choosing alpha males. Yes, women choose who (based on genes) gets to survive into the future. They get to use their super intuitive powers, as indicated by their levels of attraction, to choose the next generations, and that's just too hard for beta males to accept. It can't be right. She has to be flawed, or better yet, evil. She has to be Eve, right? Yes, she's the downfall of man. She needs guidance and education, and to be infused with the discipline of law.

This is the madness that still exists in the minds of men (and most women) to this day—that a woman's sexuality is an existential threat to humanity and our civilized culture; thus, it's invalidated. This brings us back to the Womb Choice and why it might be hard to accept that women (i.e., the feminine) can desire someone strictly for their physical attraction; there's somehow a level of wisdom inherent in that choice that is consequential to our survival as human beings. Maybe that sexual attraction indicates a real or true need she has for the sake of her health, healing, and sexual expression. Or maybe it is an indication of true, lasting relationship potential. The bottom line is that it's the foundation of our acceptance of a culture that has rejected the role of femininity and women's sexuality.

Womb Choice Quotes

If you've been Womb Chosen, you might hear some of the following quotes during your relationship.

"That's the best sex I've ever had before in my life. I thought I was going to die from coming so many times."

"I just want your dick inside of me."

"Don't stop fucking me."

"Nobody fucks me the way you do."

Carl's Story Time

My ex-girlfriend and I had a rough breakup. I basically told her I didn't want to be with her anymore, and I stopped talking to her. As we were ending our breakup discussion, she asked, "I know we're not together anymore, but can we still fuck?" That statement informed me I was a Womb Choice and that the essence of her choosing me was about me being inside her as much as possible. She didn't care about titles. She wanted access to sex. Whenever we would meet up somewhere, it was always a fuck fest. Other things didn't really matter to her, to be honest. I respected her mind and perspective on things and also wanted her to take care of me. I wanted her to suck and fuck me every day too, acknowledging I loved the fact that she loved to fuck me.

We didn't get along philosophically on some key issues, and

those issues finally reared their heads during a critical juncture of our relationship. What juncture? When we tried to live together or attempted to bring in some Support Choice energy into our relationship. The husband and wife thing wasn't going to work for us. I mean, it could have, but it wasn't something that came naturally to us, like fucking.

Another girlfriend of mine used to always talk about my penis. She wanted to fuck all the time, but she was also fascinated with different aspects of my penis. "Carl, are you circumcised? I mean, your penis is so smooth, and it feels so good when it's inside of me. Plus, it's girthy and fits inside of me just right. I can feel it pressing against every wall in my pussy when you're inside of me. I mean, to be honest, you don't even have to move inside of me. If you just sit there, I'll be able to feel you and orgasm repeatedly." We could be out having lunch or dinner, and she'd start talking about my penis and how amazing it is and asking questions about it. She would tell me repeatedly that no other man makes her feel this way during sex. These were clear indications she had Womb Chosen me, and that her craving and desire for me was sexual at its core.

Another girlfriend would tell me how she simply couldn't fuck any other man and that no penis was like mine and that she'd do whatever she needed to do to have access to my penis. She'd pay for flights, come to wherever I told her to come to, drop other guys in an instant, or even be completely submissive to me. Again, these are signs a woman has Womb Chosen you, because she's clearly prioritizing the sexual connection above all else.

Kenya's Corner

I first conceived the concept of Womb Choice after meeting a man in New York City named David. I had been married so long (12 years at the time) that I'd forgotten my womb is a living thing, choosing beyond my control the partners it wants. When I say womb, I mean the root chakra. This is a symbolic portal at the base of the spine that literally regulates our primal, sexual desire. So, when I met David at a coffee hub in Harlem, I literally felt my root chakra spin. I experienced an uncontrollable desire to have sex with him, like in the bathroom, right now, or almost immediately.

I felt caught off guard and dumbfounded. Having been married, I realized I had turned off my root chakra, exchanging its function for that of the heart chakra (i.e., parenting, mothering, and being a devoted wife). But it so happens Carl and I were now open relating—we had decided that polyamory was our way of relating—so I was free to FEEL again. What I felt in just the first five minutes of meeting this man was something that made my hormones rage and my mind foggy. How would I approach this person knowing I had already chosen him sexually?

It ended up that I did indeed approach, and although I played it cool, sliding him my business card and introducing myself, I knew that if he were to call and pursue me, there would not be anything in the way of giving my full body to this man. This is the feeling, I think, that movies and fantasy romance novels attempt to portray. Womb Choice is the hormonal cocktail that encapsulates the concept of being "in love." Falling in love is what Womb Choice feels like; it's a sexual desire that makes us believe we are on top of the world! It's like a drug of sorts.

Within a week, I was involved sexually with David. A common Womb Choice theme is sex on the first date. Things went so well with him, he chose back immediately, and we started a romance that would not end for nine years. Even today, we are still in contact—because once a Womb Choice, always a Womb Choice.

The trouble with Womb Choice is most do not understand that

this kind of relationship often houses the most powerful parental trauma. In other words, Womb Choice is a primal love that includes primal sex. The first primal love for most of us is our parents. Thus, the Womb Choice relationship offers an opening to seeing our parents reflected in the interactions. In all of my Womb Choice relationships, I saw my father and my grandfather reflected back to me. My pains and unhealed traumas from those first primal relationships (attractions) I had for my male caretakers always played out in my Womb Choice unions. One has to know how to deal with this, or THAT they are dealing with this, for the relationship to succeed.

Crown Choice

If Womb Choice is the choice to be physically dominated by a man, Crown Choice is the choice to be mentally expanded by a man. A woman is essentially looking for a man who carries the energy of the MONK archetype. Some women feel a similar sense of sexual openness with men who they know are their mental and intellectual superiors. This mental expansion also translates into their sexual lives, where these men have mastered certain techniques that can bring out a woman's deepest orgasmic state. As mentioned before, for women, sex begins in the head (i.e., crown) and the Crown Choice understands how to get her out of her head.

A Crown Choice is also someone who can help a woman grow beyond her current level of character and spiritual development. He can challenge and push her to the next intellectual level. He can also push her toward her purpose and help her understand what she's here to do and what her offerings are to the world.

In addition, there's a spiritual component to the Crown Choice. Women are the gatekeepers and guardians of spirituality and are always interested in maximizing their spiritual power and being in alignment with their highest self. What spirituality and spiritual growth are will vary from person to person; growth and expansion in that arena is the consistency we're referring to. For this reason, women often choose to be with men who they can trust to bring out these spiritual aspects within.

We need to be clear on the sexual component of the Crown Choice because the MONK is an androgynous-submissive archetype, and he somehow has women open to a similar degree as the SOLDIER, who is the Womb Choice. Being androgynous means he will be sought out and will never be the seeker for a relationship. This means you'll have to desire what he has to offer, since there won't be any pull drawing you to him. His submissive nature means you'll have to be in a mental state where you're ready to receive his gifts in order for him to choose you back. In no way can he be negotiated with or coerced because there is nothing anyone has that he really needs, outside of an audience to hear his insights.

Stereotypically, we can say the Crown Choice is the sapiosexual type of attraction, where the man's mind and thinking are the basis of her attraction. She knows he's a Crown Choice because she realizes her attraction to him after she hears him speak about a particular subject or after she reads his writing. She may see him first, but not be attracted to him until she evaluates his mind. This is the critical difference between a Crown Choice and a Womb Choice, where the latter is based on physicality.

Crown Choice Quotes

If you've been Crown Chosen by a woman, you might hear some of the following quotes during your relationship with her.

"I think you're brilliant."

"Tell me more about what you see in me."

"I really feel like you understand me. Like, the real me."

"I knew you would know the answer. You always do."

"I know I can reach my potential with you."

Carl's Story Time

If you read my book, "Finding Male Sexuality: A Personal Journey in Awakening the Masculine Sexual Self," you may remember me talking about the Tantric Goddess. I met her at our very first public tantra demonstration in Atlanta back in 2007. For those not familiar with tantra, it's basically an art and science around maximizing sex and intimacy to be a tool of physical and emotional healing and to help us manifest our desires in the world. It's taking the creative energy of sex and using it to create our lives. To do so, we need to go beyond the pornographic aspects of sex and work with its more subtle, energetic aspects.

Kenya and I had set up a great venue with a bed at the front of the room with candles, incense, and music. It had the feel of an exotic bedroom with rose petals and dimly lit lights. Our goal was to demonstrate how tantra could be used by anyone willing to try it out. We had a nice sized room and ended up hosting about seventy five people who wanted to see what we had to say. The first part of the event was a lecture about sex and tantra and how they can improve our relationships. We did some affirmations followed by a guided meditation to get everyone into the proper state of mind. Next, we moved to taking volunteers from the audience.

Our first volunteer was a sweetie. She came up and lay on the bed. I could tell she was nervous, but I was too. This was my first public demonstration of how to utilize tantra to bring about pleasure and orgasm without touch. What made it more interesting is that she was there with her boyfriend, which made it a bit awkward for both of us, to be honest. I instructed her to relax and just allow herself to feel. She closed her eyes and began to relax her muscles and slowly faded into the mattress we were both lying on. I was on my side and she was on her back. I motioned my hand to interact with her auric field and allowed her to react organically to what she felt. She began to move and adjust her body as if she was feeling sensations inside herself that she didn't quite understand. I totally invited these adjustments and reminded her to breathe naturally. She began to fight it a bit and hold back, which is understandable because we were in a public setting. There were literally over seventy people watching her. They wanted to see how she was going to react, and feeling sexual isn't always the most comfortable expression in a public setting. Either way, she was definitely able to experience sexual excitement that took her to the verge of orgasm. It was a beautiful first experience for her, and one that I felt she could build on going forward.

Now to volunteer number two: the Tantric Goddess. This woman was so beautiful, with full lips, breasts, and hips. When she walked, she did so with grace and confidence, which made her stand out in the crowd. Actually, I noticed her right away when she first walked into the event space. She was wearing a short skirt, with her hair all-natural and well-styled, and short heels. I instructed her to take her heels and jewelry off and lay on the bed. She was about five feet, two inches tall. Her skin was brown. I instructed her to take some deep breaths and relax, which she did.

I took a moment to just look at her body to gain familiarity with it, but also to marvel at her curves and softness. As she sunk into the mattress, and as her breath started to deepen and become more rhythmic, I began to touch her aura. It felt milky like the light rings around Saturn or the lightest silk imported from the finest mills in China. I imagine my energy felt electric to her because she began to move and react in time with the movement of my hand. It was like we were dancing and I was leading her to a place of pleasure and release. When I looked at her face, I could see her eyes had rolled back into her head as if she was studying her hairline. There was a bit of surprise on her face, but she wasn't able to think about what to do. She was in a state of surrender. Next, I moved my hand to her abdomen, and her body jumped like it was hit by a lightning bolt. Her head came up off the bed and then crashed back into the pillow. Then it came up again and once more crashed down into the pillow as if voltage was running through her body. The next time, her legs came up with her head, and her arms raised just above her hips. Only her ass was on the bed and she was frozen in that position for about five seconds—even though it felt like hours. She was in a state of orgasmic bliss. She surrendered to her pleasure. We continued the work for another five minutes to the total amazement of those in attendance. As she came down from her bliss, she turned and looked at me in my eyes. She was still half there and half gone into another world, but her eyes spoke to me. They said so much and showed their amazement and appreciation. What I didn't know, but what I could feel, is that she chose me at that moment. How did she choose me? It was a Crown Choice because her mind was stretched—she met someone who could expand her beyond what she previously thought was possible.

When we would eventually have sex, it was a continuation of that growth and expansion. She was enamored with the energy work and the tantric connection to pleasure and orgasm, and she saw me as a vehicle to have those experiences and understand them on a deeper level. Our sex was tantric. It was exotic. It was had with the expectation of deepening her orgasm. She made offerings of her energy and gifts in exchange for my focus on her. This is the type of sex you can expect in a Crown Choice relationship.

She was looking for me to expand her orgasm because she hadn't had one during intercourse. Part of her attraction was her belief in me to get her there. It was an inner feeling she had. I never told her I could get her there, but she had an intuitive feeling she could experience that with me. That's the basis of her choosing me as a Crown Choice—an inner knowing that I could help her expand into her sexual power as a woman.

Another girlfriend of mine was ready to take her life to the next level, but she was unsure how to do it. She needed someone who believed in her and who also had the knowledge of how to get a better corporate job while simultaneously doing some entrepreneurial work. A lot of our time would be spent talking about strategy for how to sell her services and telling her that I believed in her. After these conversations, she would tell me how much she missed me and wanted to fuck me. This is my indication I was a Crown Choice to her. It was me sharing my knowledge that made her wet for me. Sure, she was also attracted to me in other ways, but the business and spiritual coaching role I played in her life was number one for her.

Kenya's Corner

When I met my husband and co-author of this book, I knew immediately that he was my partner for life. We met at a political movie about hip hop. This was at Howard University in 1995 at the height of the hip hop revolution, where a conversation about hip hop music might lead to deeper discussions on social justice, spirituality, or even misogyny and its stronghold in the minds of men everywhere. After the movie, I distinctly recall wanting to discuss each aspect of it with him. We spent the evening deep in thought, sharing at visceral levels that spiraled deeper and deeper.

Crown Choice is the kind of connection where an all-night conversation about psychology, spirituality, and manifestation is the 'sex' that other relationship styles experience. Our sex was literally the open flow of back and forth conversions that took place each time we hung out. It got to the point where I wanted to run every thought in my brain by this man just to catch his counterpoints for the thrill and bliss of it.

Crown Choice is also a healing sensual energy; the sex after those conversations was never primal, never passionate, but more elevated, and centered in the mind and not in the genitals. Often when we had sex, there would be little movement—it was just a connection of bodies whose minds were intricately woven together like a quilt created from pieces of dreams and pieces of realities yet to manifest. Our energy was clear and visceral, centered on conversations that seemed never-ending.

Crown Choice can also be quite cozy, given the depth of understanding of one another's thoughts and ideas. I recall passersby and even close family members sharing how connected they felt Carl and I were; it's as if they could see the threads of light we had braided together in our conversations. Our deep spiritual connection was a living thing that flourished outwardly as constant touch and interaction. Emotions might flare, yet in the Crown Choice connection, there is always an intellectualized and well-executed way of handling the result. We always took ownership of our patterns, conditioning, and thoughts, and utilized spiritual modalities to see us through tough times. Meditation and objective setting were strong points between us. We would set lofty goals that we'd accomplish due to our strong belief in one another, likely via our true understanding of one another's thought processes.

Overall, Crown Choice love is a great connection for a lifelong marriage. Carl and I have been married 24 years on the day of this writing, and we still connect best and most intimately over a conversation around the state of the world. He loves to know my thoughts on things, and his thoughts always make perfect sense to me. We connect in a world beyond the physical, one that extends deep into the spiritual realm.

Our children have benefitted from our connection since it's not based on primality, but rather on spirituality. Our children have enjoyed watching as our combined energies create the reality around us in whatever ways they manifest. Our thoughts might seem unconventional, but they have worked to produce each dream we set out to realize. Over time, we've realized that even the dreams that have not yet come to pass are fully possible as long as we have one another and our celestial union—the battery which powers our dreams.

Support Choice

When a woman desires to have a man be dominant over her by keeping the relationship and family organized as well as taking accountability for it, she makes a Support Choice. She's essentially looking for a man who carries the energy of the LEADER (i.e., king) archetype. In this case, she desires to be taken care of and have the burdens of the physical world lifted from her so she can focus on other things that are important to her (i.e., having and nurturing children or self-care).

This relationship isn't about physical security and safety as much as a type of social security; when a man supports you in this way, he shields you from public critique and criticism that may question your womanhood, worth, or value. In other words, when a man says he's going to take responsibility for you in that way where he's willing to serve you, he's essentially vouching for your worthiness as a woman.

What also goes with not being the master of the external world is the desire to have a guide. It's not about helplessness, but rather about having someone support and relieve the burdens of life. Think of the Support Choice as the first line of defense against a potentially cruel world. It's just what many of us crave, especially women who desire to focus on making the magic happen, bringing the world together, or seeing a better future for the family.

Let's talk about why the Support Choice is dominant, where the woman is submissive considering she might not have a maximum level of sexual attraction to him. The Support Choice aligns with the LEADER archetype, which is generally considered to be in charge and in control of the relationship. The LEADER is essentially the primary guide and organizer of the relationship. This is the dominant skill he's cultivated and the skill his wife is submitting to—organization, guidance, presence, and leadership. His primary responsibility is to make sure his wife has what she needs to be comfortable and secure. Like they say, "Happy wife, happy life." It's the husband's "job" to facilitate his wife's happiness because that's what he's cultivated as a skill set. Any man who's been married for at least seven years knows this to be true. A lot of the relationship involves him catering to and dealing with his wife's emotional needs to keep the family and relationship on track toward its goals of raising healthy children (i.e., graduation) and securing the couple's retirement. He's not necessarily the dominant person sexually, intellectually, financially, etc., but he doesn't have to be. The Womb Choice tends to be the sexual and physical dominant. The Crown Choice tends to be the mental and intellectual dominant. The Manifestation Choice tends to be the financial dominant. The Support Choice tends to be the organizational dominant, in terms of getting the couple from point A (i.e., marriage) to point B (i.e., retirement). He keeps the family intact and on track. He holds things together and puts out fires as they arise. He provides the physical presence everyone needs to feel comfortable, safe, and protected.

A mistake that's made for men who've been Support Chosen is to assume their role in the relationship covers the areas of sex and mental domination. It doesn't. It's the slow realization of this fact that leads to married men who've been Support Chosen going out and attempting to find other women who are more into them sexually. He may be the dominant organizationally, but he is the submissive or the one who is not necessarily chosen sexually. When we observe men and infidelity and the fact they need to sneak around to get their needs met or that they can't be truthful with their wives, it's an indication they are subject to an authority figure (i.e., dominant in other areas of the relationship). Again, it's a subtle reality and not one we've been told about, but it's the truth. The men who are most successful in marriage tend to be the ones who get about their business of managing, leading, organizing, and being accountable for the family, while also accepting that they are not dominant in all areas when it comes to their wives.

We're asking everyone to take a sober view of attraction and choice. Everyone can't be everything to you. Is it possible? Technically, anything is possible, but it's highly unlikely, especially when you factor time into the equation. Things change. People change, and that includes our needs and perspectives. One of the biggest challenges with having a Support Choice is the desire for him to be your sexual god, wanting him to be someone that you're so passionately into that you can't keep your hands off him. Again, if you truly have that, more power to you, but the reality is that if he's a Support Choice, your attraction and desire for him will be average at best. It's appreciation sex, which is nothing to be ashamed of. It's sex based on the love you have for him instead of the craving in your womb. And guess what? There's absolutely nothing wrong with appreciation sex. We're not saying fuck when you don't want to fuck, but if you feel led to fuck your man out of appreciation for how he shows up for you and the family daily, then do it and feel amazing about it. It's justified. It's right. It's a part of maintaining the marathon of marriage. Don't feel guilty about not viscerally wanting your man. It's ok. Those feelings cannot be manufactured, because they're biologically based on preserving the human species rather than romance.

This brings us to the other side of the equation. If you don't want your man sexually like that, how is he going to feel? Should you lie to him? Will he lose interest in you? Will he cheat on you? It's a tough situation. Obviously, the strength of your relationship stands on your intimacy with your partner, and intimacy is based upon truthfulness. Intimacy is about being close to someone, and the only way to get them close to you is to allow them into the real you: mind, spirit, body, and belief. Once they're connected to you in these ways, you've achieved intimacy. Since truthfulness is the prerequisite to intimacy, the degree to which you and your husband can have real conversations about your sex life will be the determinant in the survival of the marriage. This means you should talk to your husband about the fact that he's a Support

Choice and explain to him what that means. Ideally, you have that conversation on day one, but better late than never. Once you have that conversation and you level with him about what your sexual needs are, you can both figure out how to address it and come up with a plan of action.

The main point of the FCP is to acknowledge the diverse needs women (i.e., feminine and submissive) have and how and why they go about meeting those needs. However, we shouldn't feel it's normal to expect to have all of our needs met by one partner. This might be one of the hardest aspects of the FCP, but one that is worth mastering. It's why we went through the GE-PR Matrix to illustrate the differences between how and why we move through the world as a basis of understanding things aren't the same. All attractions, relationships, and feelings aren't equal, and there's a really good reason why.

Let's get back to women managing their Support Choices. As we said earlier, you need to be clear in your head about why you've chosen your partner. It's also important that you communicate the reason you're with him and not lead him down a path where he thinks his sexual virility is the source of your attraction. You must maintain a level of sobriety around how you represent the relationship. It should be made clear up-front that you expect him to be there for you as an emotional support figure, a father to your children, someone who works to provide a house, and someone who is competent and responsible. You should also be clear on what you're providing and why, whether that's nurturing him, being dedicated to him, or supporting him in achieving his dreams. Doing so sets the foundation for the relationship. It's something you can fall back on as the relationship matures as a reminder for why you are together. It's not always easy to be truthful up-front out of fear of losing someone we really want to be with, unless we paint a fantasy picture of what they desire and expect. However, the crash and burn resulting from these lies is far worse than being truthful up-front.

A Support Choice also offers a level of protection and security in that she knows he has thought everything through when it comes to relationships, money, family, etc. There's a certain calmness that comes over you as a woman when you know the man you're with has literally thought about everything, which in turn allows you not to have to think so much. Again, this opportunity to not think allows a wife to be more relaxed and more orgasmic with her husband.

Another aspect to be aware of when making a Support Choice is that he should be someone who is truly supportive of the real you. It feels so much better to submit to someone who has love and respect for the real you, rather than someone you have to pretend around, like a boss or supervisor at work. We know it can be scary to put the real you out there—no one wants to be judged or possibly be rejected by someone we really like—but it pays off to do so to secure a man who's really about you. Remember, we're talking about your life partner and your king, so choose wisely because he will be the leader of the family moving forward, and he can only lead when he knows and understands the real you.

Carl's Story Time

Kenya chose me as a Crown and Support Choice. The Crown Choice was associated with the fact that we were philosophically aligned on multiple levels. The Support Choice was based on the fact that I was getting my MBA and about to work in Corporate America, and that I had a desire to be a husband and father. In addition, she saw elements of her father in me as a man. We were both fair complexioned, into computers, wore glasses, about the same height, and had a nerdy vibe about us. The fact that I reminded her of her father is a primary indicator of me being a Support Choice. I was the kind of man she could bring home to her family and say, "This is who I'm choosing for a husband," and get great feedback and approval. I was handsome, which meant the children would come out looking good. I was smart, which meant the children would come out being intelligent. I was tall, which meant I could look the part of a leader in a stereotypical sense. I was educated, which meant I would be able to support the family financially. My mother was married, which meant there would be some pressure to maintain a family. Most of all, I was a bit naive, which meant she felt she would be able to manage me inside of our relationship to fulfill her agenda of becoming a wife and mother and portraying the image of what she thought her parents wanted her to be. An important part of Support Choice energy is to not only be with someone you think is capable, but also someone you have the edge over sexually. For example, if I sexually dominated Kenya, she wouldn't be able to maximize her position as mother, queen, and matriarch in the family. Marriage isn't about sexual gratification, fun, and passion so much as realizing a dream and carrying forth a legacy. As a woman, you need to be somewhat sober mentally and emotionally to do this, and Kenya definitely had a sober perspective when it came to our relationship. I can say this compared to the other men she dated before me, who were hip hop artists and cool guys with no interest in long-term relationships or fitting into society. In other words, for the most part, I was a safe choice.

As a man, I need to take the cues of a woman's attraction for me. It's my responsibility so that I can understand how to manage the relationship and my behavior with the woman who's chosen me. If she's been around me for a while and never really expressed any physical attraction for me, but eventually seems to find me attractive, I'm probably a Support Choice. It means that after she's had time to observe me and consider me, she's decided that I would be a great partner. If upon first seeing me and having an immediate reaction or attraction, I'd be a Womb Choice. If she read a book of mine or heard me speaking about a topic with depth to it, I would most likely be a Crown Choice. If she appeared attracted to the way I'm dressed or was influenced by my car or money, I would be a Manifestation Choice. These are loose examples, but can be a part determining which choice you are as a man—in the same way that it can help women understand which choice the man is for them.

I remember after my mother got divorced how she went through a long courting process with different men. I had a chance to observe some of the men she courted and was courted by,. and was able to see the things she was considering when evaluating them. She eventually chose and married one of the men I observed, who came across as a classic Support Choice. He was well put together, in shape, had his finances in order, worked a solid job in the automobile industry, was present and protective of her, and seemed to take responsibility for his life. These were clear Support Choice characteristics and fit well with someone she'd want to be with in her life, considering she'd already been through a divorce. She was choosing a man who was better than her ex-husband in certain areas, primarily in being responsible and accountable for his life and words.

Kenya's Corner

I've had one major Support Choice over the years, and his name is Noble. From the day we met, and through today, he's been there for me emotionally, with the children, and in a submissive position with his masculinity. I am his feminine dominant. He is more than willing to take care of the things I want done, such as mowing the lawn, supporting my children, and being with me when I feel down and need a best friend kind of vibration in my life.

I wish I had known how to be a better feminine dominant to him; we struggled with the dominant and submissive because neither of us knew how to be in these positions without feeling awkward. Yet, for the most part, we were able to work through things. He lived here at the house with me and my husband (Crown Choice) and my other husband (Womb Choice). He was responsible for the duties he fulfilled. In exchange, I nurtured him, offering massage, emotional support, and food daily.

Often with Support Chosen men, there may be a sense that sex is lacking. However, sex is not the only important part of a relationship. With Support Choice, I've noticed that if the masculine can allow the feminine to dominate, there will be regular sex. However, this takes loads of work and learning how to be in the submissive and dominant.

Manifestation Choice

When a woman chooses a man who submits to her by showering her financially and materially, he's known as a Manifestation Choice. She's essentially looking for a man who carries the energy of the NEGOTIATOR archetype. This means not only financially, but also the desire to feel special inside of a relationship, which includes material gratification, affirming words, special moments, and witnessing by the public on some level.

The Manifestation Choice has always been a difficult one for women to make because of the negative connotation around loving someone strictly for their money and what they can do for you financially. As we stated earlier, it's not just about material resources, but also the desire to feel special. That being said, there is nothing wrong with being attracted to someone and desiring to be with them based on what they can do for you financially, especially when both people are supplying one another with what they want. It's no secret that many men focus on making money for the express purpose of being more attractive to women and having access to the most beautiful women in the world.

The importance is that women recognize this choice as something that is both necessary and legitimate. It's human nature to want to feel special and to experience some of the specialness and luxuries of life. There's absolutely nothing wrong with wanting this. There's also nothing wrong with wanting to share in an experience with someone else where you're the recipient of those gifts and specialness. That's why we love birthdays so much—we are made to feel special by our loved ones and peers. It's really that simple.

Again, we need to acknowledge the strength and power of the choices in how they influence us sexually. A woman's attraction for a man who's a Manifestation Choice will correspond with the things he does that are romantic, special, and cleverly spoken. This means when he's actively engaging in these activities, he will be attractive to those women who have Manifestation Chosen him. These are the activities that will allow her to be wet and excited for you. It's important for men not to be confused about why a woman's sexually attracted to you. It's not based on looks or your raw physical or sexual nature—although there may be a level of attraction in those areas. The choice represents the foundation of the sexual foundation between the couple. We can't forget that or attempt to change why we were chosen just because our egos want to be recognized for another set of characteristics of our being.

Another characteristic of the Manifestation Choice is his ability to utilize words and his gift of communication as a means of guiding, controlling, and manipulating (in a positive way) situations. The Manifestation Choice individual tends to be an expert communicator and one who understands what to say and when to get what he desires. He's also able to use his communication to soothe a woman's ego and emotions and put her at ease. He does this through comedy or compelling arguments and discussions, which allows his woman to feel comfortable, assured, and comforted when she's with him. Part of this communication involves sales, where he's able to sell a concept to her so she can visualize it and accept that vision as her reality going forward. This is not too much different from how a salesperson or politician puts an image in the minds of their customers and constituency so they can lower their defenses down and make sure they feel comfortable in what they're being sold and told.

Kenya's Corner

As a woman, I love to feel special. It's just the way it is. I like to be spoiled and treated in a way that reflects my value, and this is what I've experienced with men who I consider to be my Manifestation Choices. They're willing to go the extra mile when it comes to taking me to nice places, showing me off to the world, and saying the words I love to hear. It just feels good, and as a woman, it's something to be embraced.

It has not always easy for me to handle my Manifestation Choice men—this is due to my nature as a Monk (submissive) and double Soldier (neutral). I do not have a lot of dominant feminine energy so it's hard for me to order men around and ask for what I want materially. It feels somewhat contrived for a person like me to make sense of the idea that a man wants to take care of me financially or be submissive to me in ways that equate to material exchange.

Most often, my Manifestation Choice men have been clients. In this way, I am able to justify the spending of money on me and the use of my dominant energy as a coach. One guy I loved and held as a Manifestation Choice was a client I used to go see in Arizona. He'd pay me nearly five thousand dollars per weekend for my presence and services. This initially included coaching but expanded to childcare and tantra lessons. It felt really good to tell him what I expected. But without training from the Blue Butterfly Women of Progressive Love™ Academy, I would not have been able to ask for what I desired in a dominant way. I do look forward to attracting more Manifestation Choice men—he pampered me, bought me jewelry and clothing, and always wanted me to look and feel my best. Given I deal with lots of Womb Chosen men, it's a real treat to commune with a Manifestation Choice.

Carl's Story Time

As a man, one way to determine if you're a Manifestation Choice is based on whether you spend money on your partner. For example, I was dating a younger woman who I didn't meet in person for over five years. The essence of our relationship was talking on the phone, giving her advice, and helping her with her life and other relationships. We eventually got together when she came to visit me. We had sex, spent time together, and had great interactions. But that would be the last time we'd meet, partly because of the physical distance between us. One thing that happened in our relationship was that she started asking me for money—nothing large, just lunch here, dinner there, etc. I fell right into that role of supporting her financially in small ways, and it felt right to me. She understood how to talk to me and be that soft, beautiful energy that made me feel amazing as a man. She was able to heal me at a distance just by her voice (she's a singer too), smile, super white teeth, and her deference to me. She always made me feel like a man in charge who's wise and is to be respected. When she came to visit me, she deferred to me. She fucked and sucked me exactly like I wanted her to. Based on conversations we had throughout the years, she had super soft energy. She always dressed up to look cute, just like a princess, even when we were hanging out around the house. When we went out, she would want to take pictures and do special things. It didn't have to be expensive as long as it felt special. She loved feeling as though we had an exclusive relationship where everything we did was unique and special. Those were the keys to understanding I was a Manifestation Choice for her. Sometimes you need to take things at face value. The truth is, I was giving her money, and she showed up for me like a princess in my life.

I never felt like I was a Womb Choice because she described those men to me. She didn't really want to be a life partner of mine, so I knew I wasn't a Support Choice. She did respect my mind, though, so I may have been a Crown Choice to her as well. Here are a few more clues. Number one, she would talk about us not having sex because she said my penis was too big for her and it was uncomfortable. I've had sex with women who were super attracted to me who would work through our penis-to-vagina size ratio to make sure we kept fucking. Those were Womb Choices. Number two, she didn't press the issue to go out of her way to see me. She wanted to see me but skipped some opportunities to do so. Part of this was because of my dynamic relationship, but the other part was that her sexual passion for me was tame. Number three, she contacted me after she saw me on a television show, which made me a celebrity in her eyes—even if I was only a "C" level celebrity. Fame, specialness, and money were a prominent part of her thought process after seeing me on a popular night-time show. Number four, she had stated she wanted to be with me but had several conditions to make that happen. There's nothing wrong with conditions, but when someone Womb Chooses you, they tend to focus on being with you first and then figuring out the details later. These were just a few clues to help me understand how I was chosen and thus how I should show up for her and our relationship.

Soul Choice

Sometimes, a woman chooses a man based on what he's about more than who he is. It's his mission and calling in life that she's drawn to, and she sees herself doing the work with him. This type of attraction goes beyond superficial physical traits, money, or anything that could generally be considered as changeable. It goes to causes and inner callings that speak to a person's incarnation work, as indicated by their spiritual makeup. His calling and work revealed her attraction to him and that is what she is married to—not the man. If he were to stop doing that work or change his calling, she would cease to be drawn to him and continue to do the work, or find another man with an equally powerful, soulful calling.

The soul level calling is a sense of the authentic vibration of the man. It's a way to know the deepest aspect of who he is, as indicated by his dedication to his mission. Because we're talking about a soul level attraction, we're also talking about a deeply intimate connection, which is the foundation of her closeness to him as well as her sexual attraction for him. She can feel his soul by opening up her soul to connect to his, which by default is an orgasmic experience. This soul level sexual attraction is felt as energy, vibration, and a consciousness-connecting experience. It's almost the opposite of carnal, which is the basis of Womb Choice sexual attraction. It's different from Support Choice attraction, which is based on duty and an ability to protect and provide. It's different from Crown Choice attraction, which is based on an ability to help a woman expand and grow beyond her current level of spirituality and acculturation. It's different from Manifestation Choice attraction, which is based upon an ability to make a woman feel special, desired, and adored. Again, the idea here is to tap into a man's core calling and love what he represents as a manifested mission-being on the planet.

What separates the Soul Choice from the other choices is that it can also fit into the Desire Paradigm, as well as outside of all paradigms, because it is more about the mission than the person. Someone could choose themselves as a Soul Choice, or anyone for that matter, but it still wouldn't be about the person per se. Another way to say it is the Soul Choice isn't a feminine or submissive choice; rather, it is one that aligns with both the androgynous gender energy and the neutral position. Therefore, this type of choice isn't recognized in the romantic and relationship spheres in the same way, because the focus on partnership is secondary.

Carl & Kenya's Story Time

When we first constructed the FCP, there was no Soul Choice. Because of this, we primarily identified our relationship as a Crown Choice because we were aligned philosophically. We learned from each other and grew as a result of listening to one another. Over time, however, it became evident that our mission was a central part of our connection and our reason for being together. Let's try to explain.

Early in our relationship, we did meditations and past life regression work to see about our past connections so we could know why we were together in this lifetime. One of our past lives was Kenya and I as brother and sister in a land that we identified as somewhere on the continent of Africa. During this time, there was an imminent threat of invasion by Europeans from the north. Well, let's just say that we were aware of the imminent threat; however, that wasn't the case among everyone else. We saw an opportunity to do something necessary—to expand the consciousness of our people. What does that mean? It means to create an experience that would help us come into a higher understanding of ourselves as spiritual beings and give us access to parts of our consciousness that we once had before devolving into our current condition. At one time, we were priests and metaphysicians in Kemet, creating universes, manipulating earthly forces, and traveling interdimensionally. However, those days had long passed and we only had access to but a tiny percentage of that wisdom—just enough to be ignorant and use it against one another. In other words, we were lost as a people. We stopped our expansion. We ceased to grow, evolve, and elevate ourselves into our potential. That brought us back to the imminent interaction with what would soon be European invaders from the north. We did a series of rituals to facilitate the North Atlantic slave trade as a vehicle to elevate the consciousness of our people. We all know the history that follows. As a result of that ritual, we needed to incarnate inside of it so we could experience it for ourselves.

Kenya incarnated as a woman who was a slave and was being held for sex. I incarnated as a man who was a slave leading a rebellion, only to realize that the forces working against us were too great. Thus, I sacrificed myself and decided to incarnate in the future to fight another day. This past life experience brings us both to our current lives as teachers and founders of the Progressive Love™ Academy. For us, Progressive Love is a movement to wake up the consciousness of the entire planet. It's bigger than just a business for us. It's what we would do whether we were together or not, but our being together is what facilitated the movement to take place. Thus, we could easily say our relationship is based on a Soul Choice dynamic. Did she choose me as a Soul Choice? Sure, but I would say it was a subconscious thing. Did I choose her as a Soul Choice? Sure, but again it was naturally subconscious.

What was also interesting about Kenya and I coming together was how it happened. We met on a blind date when we were both in college at Howard University. I was in graduate school earning my MBA and she was in undergraduate school earning a degree in Early Childhood Psychology. She lived in the same building as one of my good friends, and he saw her one day and tried to talk to her. He was attracted to her and was hoping to get her number and move things forward, but there was a problem—he had a girlfriend, and Kenya knew her. So, when he approached Kenya she said, "Aren't you dating my neighbor, Irene?" When she said this, he quickly pivoted and said he was only talking to her because he thought she'd be a good match for his friend. Leading up to this point, Kenya had been doing rituals at the river to meet her husband. She talks more about the process in her book "Change Your Man: How to Become the Woman He Wants."

During this time, I was kind of in a dry period when it came to dating. The women in Washington, DC proved to be way different than the scores of women I had dated in North Carolina the previous five years. The women in North Carolina were fun, down to earth, and down for the hookup. Meanwhile, the women in Washington, DC were on the money and status bandwagon, which put me out of the dating game when it came to the fine women. Anyways, one day I remember having a clear vision of my wife. I was walking one night and it hit me. She was about five feet or so, thin build, brown skin, and with a short haircut. A few weeks later, I saw Kenya and her all-female band playing a concert on Howard's campus. They were good and fun to watch. Later that day, I saw her bandmate Maya in front of my dorm. She seemed to match the vision I had perfectly, so I approached her and gave her my number. She never called me. I guess I wasn't her type. Fast forward a few weeks, Keith called me saying he had a girl he wanted me to meet and that he hooked up a date night for us all. I told him I was down, and that's where I eventually met Kenya. She was the bass player from the band Soulfood Symphony. Two months later we were engaged, and ten months after that we were married. The moral of the story is that our coming together was "otherworldly," which was a further clue that it was meant to be.

A few weeks after getting engaged, we went for counsel with some priestesses of a spiritual community that we would eventually become members of. They did a reading on our relationship and got Ausar Tu Tchaas, Tehuti Hetep. The counsel they gave said that our relationship was of a high order and that we had serious work to do together in this lifetime. They said our union wasn't about our ego, but rather us elevating our consciousness to make things work. Again, this was another indicator our relationship wasn't about us; it was about the mission. The foundations of many relationships are about money, happiness, family, career, etc., but ours was about doing some serious work together. Yes, we would have all of those things, but they wouldn't be the foundation of our union. At least, not in this lifetime.

Mix & Match

One of the biggest questions we get about the FCP is whether a man can be more than one choice. For that matter, can he be all four choices at once? #lmao. The simple answer is sure, he can be more than one. It's common for us to identify a choice combination at play. For example, my wife and I are probably 50% Soul Choice, 30% Crown Choice, and 20% Support Choice. Another common combination we see with our clients is husbands being 50% Support Choice and 50% Crown Choice, or 50% Support Choice and 50% Manifestation Choice. But first, let's take some time to understand something—when we see a combination, it usually comes after the First Choice™. For example, you initially saw your man as a good husband, and over time you were drawn to his mind and wisdom. Or maybe you picked him as a Womb Choice and after ten years of marriage, you started to appreciate and acknowledge the fact that he works well with children, so you make him 70% Womb Choice and 30% Support Choice. It usually happens like this since initial attractions are very specific and that's where the intelligence is. What happens after is why we try to force our attraction into a box that makes sense to us rather than just accepting things for what they are (i.e., I'm with him because the dick is amazing).

So, can a man be all four choices? We say no, but we also know many women deeply desire this because of our culture of monogamy, where we need a one-size-fits-all kind of relationship. Also, because we have a tough time with radical honesty, it's hard for us to tell our partners we don't have that visceral sexual attraction to them. We understand that because real conversations weren't had upfront, now everyone's ego hangs in the balance. To help people learn to communicate authentically in relationships, we wrote "UPLVL Communication™: The Ultimate Solution to Eliminating Hurtful, Meaningless, and Damaging Arguments." So, we get it. We recommend you first make this assessment for your knowledge and gratification, and then decide on how you want to communicate with your partner. First, understand why you chose your partner as a tool for navigating the relationship. Next, understand why your partner has chosen you back and what they're primarily looking for in the relationship so you can give that to them.

It should also be noted that as a man, you can't change a woman's view of you. This means you can't force yourself to be seen as a particular choice. Most men I talk to want to be seen as a Womb Choice to all women, and they think they can change how a woman sees them by talking differently, lifting weights, buying a luxury car, etc. Choice doesn't work that way. It's not necessarily a conscious thing. If it was logical, choosing would only be governed by the masculine and dominant principles, which is not the case. Even if one thousand women Womb Choose you, it doesn't mean the next woman will do the same. She might not choose you at all, or choose you as a Manifestation Choice, etc. Again, it's not a logical process, which is why men have a hard time with the Feminine Choice Paradigm as a concept. It's also why many men have a hard time knowing when they've been chosen, since it's not necessarily based on something they can tangibly point to. Sometimes it is, but not always.

The First Choice™

Let's go a bit deeper into why the initial reason for choosing your partner is important. Indeed, things change over time as our priorities change or as we travel through various stages of life with our partners. Still, the initial reason for choosing your partner will always reign supreme and dictate whether you will continue to be attracted to them. This means one of the primary indicators of attraction is your sexual draw to your partner. The FCP simply helps women understand why this attraction exists. The same can be said with the Masculine Desire Paradigm (MDP), where a man's desire to experience a certain feeling can be placed in specific categories. When we say feeling, we're talking about an actual physical, visceral reaction within our bodies that proves the attraction exists, even though reactions will vary from choice to choice. That being said, the very first choice is the foundation for the relationship into perpetuity.

When the initial attraction is broken, the sexual connection and the relationship itself die. When the initial choice tenets are violated, the attraction begins to wane within the person making the initial choice. The relationship itself may still survive, but it will only be a shell of its former self. It will lack passion and possibly intimacy, and carry a level of emptiness going forward. We call this principle in relationships the First Choice™, and it's a critical litmus test for the health of the relationship. For example, a woman may choose a man as a Womb Choice, which means that having access to him sexually is critical. Maybe her choice is based on his physique or sexual prowess. The truth is, she may not know why she's sexually attracted to him in the way she is, but if that attraction point changes or goes away, it will affect her ability to continue to be drawn to him in the same way.

Let's say he loses his physique or can't keep an erection anymore; in these instances, we can safely say that the relationship will suffer because the foundational choice and attraction aren't being honored. This is different from a woman who Support Chooses her man. In this case, as long as he's showing up responsibly, providing for the family, being present with her, building family, staying presentable, etc., he can lose his physique or even have erectile problems and she'll still be drawn and attracted to him. In other words, his sexual prowess isn't the foundation of the relationship. This can be tough to accept for men and women alike because most of us try to intellectualize attraction. We think because someone is saying or doing all the right things, being responsible, or spending money on us that we'll always be attracted to them and the relationship will be solid, but that's not how it works. The Feminine Choice Paradigm defines the needs of our feminine and submissive natures, and those aspects of our being must be fed to survive in the same way that we need food to keep our physical bodies alive. Our desire to feel as described by the MDP is real and part of the foundation for why we have incarnated on the planet. We deeply crave the experience of feeling our inner emotions through our connection to the feminine and submissive principles in the world. Our masculine and dominant nature need and require this to survive and be fulfilled as the complex and divine beings we are. If a woman Manifestation Chooses a man because he says all of the things that make her feel special, spends money on her, and honors birthdays and vacations, those things cannot change, even if he suddenly becomes a sex god in the bedroom. In other words, choices rarely change on a genuine level with the same person you've already chosen. This fact contradicts what our egos would like to believe. Instead of accepting the choice from others, we'd rather have our current partner choose us in a way that's convenient for us. It's just not how it works. If as a man you've been Manifestation Chosen by your current partner but would like the experience of being Womb Chosen, you must allow the choice to come from another woman; otherwise, your feelings and ego will be hurt.

Use the descriptions of the FCP, MDP, and 9 Expressions of Love to determine why you're choosing your partner or why you've been chosen. Once you've made a determination, feel free to discuss it with your partner to see if it makes sense to both of you. If so, record it as the foundation of the relationship, and make sure you both honor it from now to eternity to help your relationship thrive.

Why the Feminine Choice Paradigm is Elusive

The concepts around feminine and submissive choice being valid are elusive because we live in a culture of monogamy and religion, which says that desire and attraction are mostly irresponsible and superficial and are therefore optional. The dominant view is that there's only one dignified reason to choose a partner—marriage. Sure, marriage can be based on romantic love and have sexual attraction, but these aspects are nice to have. What's more important is responsibility and functioning like mature adults, which means going beyond other desires we may have. That's also the solution for adultery—to just ignore those feelings and temptations and stay faithful to your partner. The other element that makes the concept of "choice" difficult to understand and believe is that religion makes sex and attraction a sin and thus something to be avoided. Overall, people feel shame for feeling sexually attracted to others even when they are single. However, once they are in a committed relationship, sexual attraction should be turned off; otherwise, religion says we are living a lustful life and are mired in sin. The combination of the culture of monogamy and religion makes it hard to be genuinely feminine or express submissive tendencies or desires. Thus, to expand our understanding of how we're feeling and why we feel that way, we must resolve the lies told to us by these two institutions: monogamy and religion.

The Rise of Monogamy & Religion

We can't discuss the current narrative of partner selection without first acknowledging the role religion has played in how we relate here in the West. For example, at the core of Christianity is the story of Adam and Eve, where Eve essentially damns the entire human race through her irresponsible and reckless choice to eat from the Tree of Knowledge. Whether we want to acknowledge it or not, this story is widely accepted as truth in Western culture even to "non-believers," labelling women as sloppy, careless, and promiscuous, even though there is no overt reference to sexuality. However, it's implicitly understood that Eve couldn't handle the glorious freedom existing in her nakedness in the Garden of Eden and was thus forced to be clothed into eternity. Another way to state it is that freedom of choice left in the hands of a woman will lead to the wrath of God. The subconscious impact of this story is that women may feel unsure about themselves, their judgment, and the trust their spouses, friends, and family have in them.

Another impactful story in Christianity involves the conception of Jesus taking place without sexual intercourse, which further demonizes women in that the most important figure to ever be born upon planet Earth has come through the birth canal but not through the act of sex that all adults so desperately crave. The implication is that the pureness of a woman is found in her virginity, meaning her desire for sex or partnership should be tamed and suppressed at all costs for the sake of humanity.

In the end, the message being communicated is that women can't be trusted with their own sexuality or to select a mate. They can't even express their attraction or desire for someone without it being some sort of violation of human purity. This further pushes women away from their desire and ability to choose a partner and closer to waiting to be selected by men. This subconscious shame also upholds the institution of monogamy by further locking women in a cage of non-expression. Monogamy as an institution becomes the final nail in the coffin when it comes to women's desires—which to some may not sound bad because it inherently supports marital fidelity. The only problem is that human beings aren't monogamous; thus, when a woman's feelings come up, she's forced to bury them in shame rather than share them with her husband or friends.

The Imbalanced Patriarchy

Another factor that makes the FCP hard to accept is the fact that we live in a broken, male-dominated society. Broken means that our society isn't focused on masculine development for men; thus, many adult males don't express their actions in a balanced, masculine way. They haven't learned to face their fears, sacrifice for something bigger than themselves, or be leaders. This is a problem because it allows men to avoid their fears when interacting with the feminine principle. As a result, men attempt to have an advantage over women by shaming them into submission and discrediting their choices, desires, and sexual expression as a way to control them, instead of honoring their organic desires. This is how men keep women boxed inside of marriage and sexually fidelitous throughout their lives. As stated earlier, this is how underdeveloped males (i.e., beta males) ensure they have access to sex and a life mate without the need to develop their masculinity. A woman's choice will tell you where you're at as a man because her attraction is organic and raw and without a plan per se, which is why we see beautiful women with average looking men. A woman's choice follows the truth of her attraction, which isn't based on superficial things or logic. It's based on the truth of a feeling.

The problem isn't with patriarchy in and of itself, because there's nothing wrong with this, just like there's nothing wrong with matriarchy. The problem is when the masculine principle is underdeveloped, which will in turn warp these institutions into something abusive and unsustainable. A balanced patriarchy will acknowledge the masculine, androgynous, and feminine elements, and create a culture where they can all be expressed. In addition, a balanced patriarchy will recognize the need for dominance, submission, and neutrality.

The Masculine Desire Paradigm™

One of the confusing things about the FCP is that it doesn't leave much room for men (or anyone in their masculine or dominant energy) when it comes to mate selection in relationships. Still, nothing can be further from the truth. The FCP simply says that women choose men to support them in manifesting their inner desire into physical reality in the world. It's considered as a choice because she's looking for that one man who can match her vision; thus, she chooses him when she finds him. Men, on the other hand, are searching for a woman to help them experience their inner feelings on a deeper level. This doesn't require one special woman to help a man, because most women are in touch with their feelings enough to guide a man on this type of journey.

It all boils down to the question of, "What do men want?" Men are searching for themselves in women, but specifically, they are looking to feel their inner power and freedom and experience devotion (i.e., care) and love (i.e., acceptance). That's it. That's all men are looking for in their connection and relationships with women. We know it's super abstract and hard to grasp, but it's the truth. Not only is it hard for women to understand, but it's also extremely hard for men to grasp. This could explain why men never seem to be satiated when it comes to sex and relationships—they don't know what they're looking for on a deep level. In other words, men are so detached from their inner feelings that they don't even know they can't feel them. They don't know they're even there. All men know is that relating with women makes them feel something so internally powerful that the only thing stronger than their desire to feel is their fear of it.

The MDP covers both the desires of the masculine and the

dominant natures of men (or anyone manifesting these energies at a particular time). The following is a summary of masculine desires.

Power Desire

When men desire to feel internally powerful without the need to show that power through force, coercion, or action, this is a feminine expression of energy where one simply knows they can manifest their lives through a sheer inner knowing that it will happen. We're talking about the ability to shape our outside reality using our internal wherewithal and conviction—nothing more, nothing less. As men, we know we have that power somewhere within us, but we are still more comfortable using force. We are still more comfortable being hands on and making things happen on our time rather than allowing our internal power to move things in its own time.

How do we experience this from a woman? We allow ourselves to not only witness it within her by maintaining proximity to her, but also by experiencing firsthand how she utilizes her power to influence our lives. She uses her power to make us orgasm during sex. She uses her power to make us consider her in everything we do. She uses her power to make us do what she wants and desires. We find ourselves subjected to it, yet we don't have a complete understanding of it. We know that to be outside of the influence of her power, we must separate from her emotionally and physically. It actually takes force in an equal and opposite direction to escape her influential power.

Again, these are subconscious desires playing out as attraction and desire; therefore, the conscious recognition of why the attraction is there or what the man is really seeking isn't always apparent. The result can be a denial of the attraction, fear of committing to the unknown, or anger toward the object of desire.

Carl's Story Time

When I was dating Diamond, I would move to her church and state to see her, be with her, get in that pussy, hear her voice, and just be in her presence. I took risks, lied to folks, spent money I didn't have, and acted low-key and reckless. She had me. Something about her had me feeling that way about her, had me wanting her, and had me jealous as fuck when she was with another man even though I was married and dating other women. She not only had the power to crush my insides with her words and actions, but also had the power to make me feel invincible. It was how she moved, cried, and spoke my name during sex. I felt powerful as a man during our lovemaking, but I also felt her power as she moved me at her will and command.

Our lovemaking would literally break me down to the point that I was experiencing and seeing a part of myself I hadn't seen before. It was a more vulnerable side of me, just like my chest was split wide open, and even though it felt strange and uncomfortable, it released a power within me that I could use in the world. It increased my inner confidence as a man. There was so much I did with her and for her that would have otherwise been impossible without that increased inner confidence (i.e., power). When I was in the vortex of relating to her, it didn't seem so bad. It didn't seem out of line or beyond my capabilities, but it was. It wasn't until I was out of the relationship, healed up, and disconnected from her that I could look back and rationally evaluate my behavior. I nearly lost so much because I was singularly focused and moving in one specific direction. Was it a bad thing? Not necessarily, especially if we were going to stay together.

But once I wasn't with her anymore, I had to play cleanup with my other relationships and areas of my life. This is power—the ability to defy all odds without care, worry, or concern, and the ability to move toward a goal so confidently that you don't even need courage since fear isn't a factor. This was my desire to feel powerful being fulfilled through my relationship with Diamond.

Freedom Desire

Women are the owners of spirituality, luck, favor, and magic. Still, these modalities are a part of a mindset and lifestyle that require a level of detachment from the physical world and its rules and restrictions. In other words, you can't be magical if you're acknowledging the power of logic and physical constructs as the dominant forces that influence reality. A part of your consciousness must go beyond reality as the masses of people accept it. This kind of freedom from the physical aspects of life is an inner desire men want to experience. Again, women (or the androgynous-submissive principle) are what's required to operate within this reality. The ability to not look for anything beyond what the environment has to offer—which includes its magical and metaphysical components, along with one's willingness to submit to these cosmic laws and influences—is what's required to live this lifestyle. Men who find themselves using force and dominance to live their lives and influence their reality find it hard to access these cosmic influences; thus, they have a subconscious draw to connect with women who are inside of this mental dynamic.

Carl's Story Time

Dating Edrea gave me a feeling of freedom. It was almost like dropping out of society and living in a love bubble. She loved to float around the country, avoid responsibility, smoke weed, sing, and avoid anything that tied her down to a monotonous lifestyle. She was intoxicating. Sex and head were epic and mind-blowing on all levels. She made the pain go away. She made me want to walk away from my life and just exist in the world, and somehow I felt things would work out, like money, sustenance, etc. Her entire life seemed to be one big adventure moving here and there, and although some parts of her life were considered a mess, being with her made it all feel viable and attractive, especially if I got to do it with her.

One of the best aspects of being with her was she was always down for whatever ideas I had. In her mind, everything I wanted to do was possible, and she enjoyed coming up with ideas that supported my dreams. I can't tell you how amazing it is to feel that you have someone in your corner who believes in all of your ideas and speaks encouraging words in the process.

Devoted Desire

Men desire to feel devotion, which is to have someone bonded to us and willing to show up and take care of us. This also includes someone who's devoted to our goals and dreams, regardless of how crazy they may sound. This is synonymous with a mother's love for their child. Although men come into adulthood, the truth is, it's impossible to separate from the desire to feel connected to devoted energy with a woman, especially when it reflects the way we were nurtured by our mothers and other women who cared for us unconditionally. A man will always desire to have a woman in his life who's in his corner, can bring him back from failure and defeat, and lift him back into his strongest self.

A man also desires to view a woman in an exalted way, just like a son looks at his mother—a queen acknowledged by the community at large that we have a unique connection too. A queen's devotion stands apart from that of other women, as it brings out our inner king energy.

As we go into the world looking for a wife, subconsciously we're looking for a woman to hold up as royalty. It completes our desire to maintain a cycle of life that started with our mothers. This energy is not sexual in nature, but rather one of respect and honor, satisfying an inner need to stand in deference to the highest feminine principle since our inception. Many men experience a lack of sexual desire over the length of their marriage because the core attraction to their wives is rooted in the desire to hold a woman up as untouchable. It's similar to how Christianity regards the Virgin Mary as a sexless, sinless member of the community such that only God has the authority to have intercourse with her. We're not saying there's no sexual attraction present; rather, there often is an internal, subconscious conflict in how men interact with their wives. From the woman's side, she might observe a lack of aggression from her husband, particularly after the marriage vows have been said. She's seeking passion and aggression from her husband but finds it's a struggle to attain.

This also explains why men often find it hard to accept that their wives might have sexual desires period, let alone desires for other men. It just violates the majestic image men hold their wives to. This is the source of the pain and heartache some men experience at the thought of their wives with another man, whether in the present, future, or past. Yes, it's true that the image of your wife with someone in the past can be hurtful, which is why the conversation around "body count" comes up in the dating and courting process. It's a sure sign that a man is considering a woman to be the queen in this life.

Love Desire

Men desire to feel love in the romantic sense, but what exactly is love? There are so many different definitions and versions of love. Still, for the sake of this book, we're talking about romantic love, which is defined as the experience of recognizing a unique quality within someone that makes them stand out from others. It's the act of recognizing the specialness within someone such that they get special time, energy, gifts, offerings, and words as indications of this love. Romantic love separates the object of this love from all others on earth and puts them in a special category. Romantic love is felt from the heart and is carried around internally as if it's an actual organ, like the lungs or liver.

Men who experience romantic love affirm their value as human beings, which can translate into resource attainment and gaining favor among peer circles. Romantic love is an expression of specialness that says who you are, what you've accomplished, your potential, and the skills you've acquired are to be admired and acknowledged.

When I was dating Monie, she would always tell me how special I was and that she believed in me. She saw talent in me and always believed I would do great things. She loved me for my unique talents and expressions and never hesitated to let me know. It helped me believe in myself. I could even say it instilled confidence in me because she was acknowledging things that others weren't saying to me or recognizing.

Soul Desire

Soul Desire for the masculine and Soul Choice for the feminine are the same because they both fall under the androgynous-neutral gender energy and position. This describes the masculine desire for connection based on an alignment of purpose and mission, where the feminine is also about the same mission. In this case, there's no need for motivating your partner to do the work because your passion is equal.

The Castigation of Masculine Sexual Desire

Again, some of these concepts about men's desire to experience specific feelings and emotions might be difficult for many of us to relate to, whether we're women or men. When you look at men's stereotypical behavior, it doesn't look like someone attempting to feel on a deeper level. It doesn't look like someone wants to see their internal power manifest in the world or to get closer to their mother's love or a desire to hold women in high exaltation. Instead, it looks more like men wanting sex at any cost, including lying for it. It looks like men playing games and sometimes playing women and other times acting irresponsibly. It looks like men attempting to escape responsibility and commitment and continue to have fun and play the field. Trust me, I get all of that, but what I'm saying is that this is what a man's search for the fulfillment of these desires looks like. It's sloppy. It's reckless. It's immature and even damaging. Why? Again, because he's not even aware that he's on this journey, which is the reason for this book. We're trying to shed light upon why a woman (i.e., the feminine and submissive principles) chooses partners and the source of her attractions. We're trying to shed light upon why a man (i.e., the masculine and dominant principles) desires to be with certain women and why he functions the way he does during the mating, dating, and courting process.

Yes, he wants sex, but that's just the surface of it. Sex is the vehicle men use to experience depth of emotion and depth of connection. It's the one consistent physical stimulus that can bring forth our love and ability to feel inside our emotional body. Sex is the one physical activity that can emotionally connect us to another human being, and bring out our desires to protect. As indicated in the masculine desires, sex is also a man's gateway to feeling his power, freedom, love, and devotion. I'm saying sex is the gateway, not the end all, be all. Being inside of a woman is analogous to being able to touch her inner emotional body and thus experience that ourselves. It's the journey to discover parts of our inner feminine and submissive selves.

Men need to have that knowledge; otherwise, we vilify ourselves as being carnal, uncaring beings who are simply looking for sensual gratification, and that couldn't be further from the truth. Yes, we want sexual gratification, but we also want an emotional connection. We want to feel on a deep level. This is our true desire, even though the thought of it doesn't sound appealing, and even though the journey itself will be one of the most challenging of our lives.

When we look at the FCP juxtaposed with the MDP, we have the following diagram illustrating how each choice and desire aligns with one another.

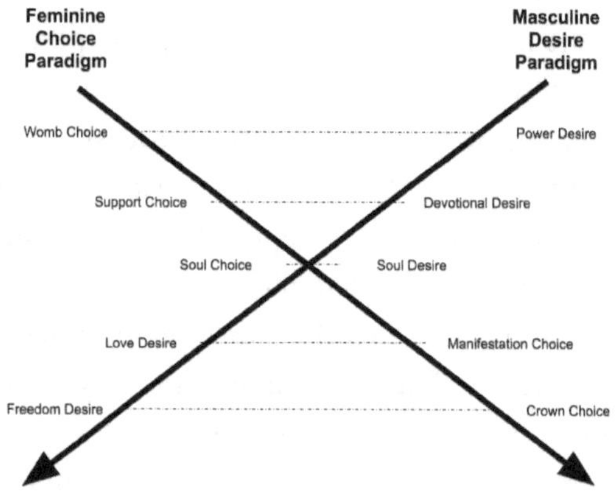
Feminine Choice Paradigm
Masculine Desire Paradigm
Womb Choice
Power Desire
Support Choice
Devotional Desire
Soul Choice
Soul Desire
Love Desire
Manifestation Choice
Freedom Desire
Crown Choice

The Illusion of Hypergamy

We need to address one more popular cultural narrative, which is the concept of hypergamy: the action of marrying up to a superior class or position. This term has been most often used in reference to women, but rarely for men. The belief is that women will, in most cases, leave their current partners if they have a realistic opportunity to mate with another person of a higher class, financial status, or masculine stature. The cultural narrative attempts to paint women as naturally hypergamous, which is why we must address it in this book. Just like the Masculine Desire Paradigm, the Feminine Choice Paradigm is not about hypergamy. Instead, the Feminine Choice Paradigm is about women being attracted to men and choosing them based on certain internal qualities they possess. Women will indeed leave men for other men, but that is a symptom of monogamy and capitalism. Monogamy is relevant because women are only allowed to have one mating experience at a time; thus, to have a different experience (not necessarily a better or higher experience), a woman will have to leave her current partner to be with a new partner. As human beings, we're not monogamous; otherwise, we would only mate once in our entire life, even if our current partners died. Instead, we are serial polyamorists at the very least and fully open at our most. Serial polyamory is the proper term to use instead of the popular "serial monogamy." Monogamy means one, while polyamory means many. So, in modern Western culture, we tend to date multiple people throughout our lives; however, those professing to be monogamous simply date one at a time (i.e., serially).

The role of capitalism is simple. Capitalism does the following:

- Puts value on everything; thus, people will be assigned a relative value. It's human nature to want to align ourselves to the highest-value people we can for our very survival and self-esteem. This creates the concept of hierarchy, elevating some over others, which in turn creates jealousy, envy, and competition.
- Introduces competition where the strong will survive and the weak will starve. Strength in modern society is often measured monetarily and through the perceived virility of one's genes.
- Eats based on effort. This means in a capitalistic society, your lifestyle and ability to feed yourself will depend upon your efforts, strategic alignments, and what moves you can make throughout your life to better position yourself for resource attainment. Thus, all participants in capitalistic culture (i.e., anyone living in modern culture) are looking for better opportunities to secure their future, as there are no guarantees or sureties.
- Creates the concept of scarcity, thus further solidifying the concept of hierarchy.

In short, women are not hypergamous any more than men are. For example, any man will leave their current job if they could double their salary. We've seen plenty of men leave their current partner for one who they consider much more attractive, younger, or more sexually exciting. Are these hypergamy examples? Sure, but it's really just the display of human nature (regardless of sex) playing out in a monogamous, capitalistic system. That's all.

Bringing it All Together

We've introduced so many concepts, but the question is: How does everything work together? Does it work together? Everything does work together, and each concept can be used individually as well. Feel free to use the 9 Expressions of Love to gauge what you or prospective partners are looking for in terms of showing their love. Feel free to use the Gender-Energy Position-Role Matrix to understand where you or your partner stands relative to their behavior, or why they may function the way they do in relationships. Use the Feminine Choice Paradigm to communicate why you're attracted to someone and what the foundation of the connection is, as well as to be clear on what your deal breakers are inside the relationship. Use the Masculine Desire Paradigm to understand what you're looking to experience emotionally and why you might be looking for specific partners to give you that experience. The Masculine Desire Paradigm can also help you understand why you may be developing very specific parts of your masculine or dominant identity in hopes of being chosen by someone who will ultimately give you the emotional experience you're looking for. All of these concepts work together seamlessly but work just as well apart. So it's up to you how you'd like to apply them in your life. The good thing about having these tools and concepts at your fingertips is that some may be easier to apply than others in certain situations. This leaves you with some choices and leverage for the many scenarios you may encounter along your relationship journey.

About the Authors

Kenya K. Stevens, founder and CEO of JujuMama, considers herself a Love Shaman. She is a relationships expert, love coach, best-selling author, wife, and mother of three. Kenya attended Howard University in Washington, D.C., where she graduated in 1997 with a degree in Education/Child Psychology. Not only did she scoop up a degree, but she also met and married a fellow Howard student, Carl Stevens. Carl and Kenya have been married for over twenty four years and now live in the mountains of North Carolina.

Carl E. Stevens, Jr., also known as Rakhem Seku, is a relationship expert, life coach, best-selling author, husband, and father of three. Carl is also the co-founder with Kenya of the Progressive Love™ Academy, an online relationships and empowerment school designed to support people in creating the life, love, and marriages they desire. Carl has two degrees: one from North Carolina State University (NCSU) in Industrial Engineering, and one from Howard University, an MBA with a finance concentration.

Beyond their college degrees, Kenya and Carl have over ten years of formal training in yoga, breathing, meditation, and metaphysical thought. They use these disciplines to formulate their unique coaching style. In 2005, Carl and Kenya co-founded JujuMama. Using the skills and unique empowerment tools they refined for years, the Progressive Love™ Movement and Progressive Love™ Academy was formulated in 2007, after broad success in coaching couples and saving marriages since JujuMama's inception.

The Stevens reach individuals deeply, supporting them in creating harmonious relationships and achieving life desires. Utilizing JujuMama's success, Kenya and her husband, Carl, have expanded the Progressive Love™ Academy into a powerful resource for coaches and couples! They have created the first relationship academy that provides a platform for their certified coaches to teach. Over 250 love coaches, tantra practitioners, and manifestation coaches have been certified through the Progressive Love™ Academy. With a flailing 55% divorce rate, the pair is sure we need new alternatives. Carl and Kenya believe Progressive Love™ can save the modern relationship.

One alternative style that the Stevens believe is aiding couples in becoming more authentic is Freedom Based Relating, or Polyamory. The couple has curated a vast library of content covering topics such as love, sex, relationships, tantric sex, metaphysics, astrology, and more. The Stevens have been featured in EBONY Magazine (February 2010 & November 2011), The Mo'Nique Show™, The Michael Baisden Show™, Fox News, Dr. Phil Show™, Rikki Lake Show™, The Brian Cunningham ShowTM, and over 300 talk radio and blog shows.

Carl E. Stevens, Jr. is also a metaphysician, and he teaches the Bagua Astrology System and applies metaphysical concepts to support people in creating the lives they desire through the Progressive Love™ Academy.

Carl and Kenya are also the authors of:

- *UPLVL Communication™: The Ultimate Solution to Save Relationships and Eliminate Hurtful, Damaging, & Meaningless Arguments*

Carl is the author of numerous books, including:

- *The Art of Open Relating: Volume 1 – Theory, Philosophy, & Foundation*
- *Tame Your Woman: Become the Man She Needs*

- *Manifesting Marriage for Women: 9 Steps to Finding Your Partner and Creating a Successful Marriage*
- *I Create My Life: Manifesting Your Desires Using the Sun Cycle*
- *Bagua Astrology Oracle Interpretation Guide*
- *Bagua Astrology Character Mapping Interpretation Guide*
- *Bagua Character Map: Science, Analysis, & Interpretation*
- *Moon Manifestation System Workbook & Journal*
- *Bagua Astrology for Beginners*

Kenya is the author of:

- *Change Your Man: How to Become the Woman He Wants*
- *Memoir of an Opening Marriage* (coming soon)

At the Progressive Love™ Academy, students are certified in the many disciplines Carl and Kenya have created and authored, including:

- UPLVL Communication™ Certification
- Life & Love Coaching Certification
- Feminine Power Certification
- i2Tantra Certification
- Moon Manifestation System Certification
- Bagua Astrology System Certification
- Three-Way Mirror Certification

Carl and Kenya have hundreds of audios and videos available to their students at the Progressive Love™ Academy, and additional products are available to the general public through their store.

To contact Kenya and Carl, you can email them at: mail@jujumama.com.

You can find their Facebook fan page at:
http://www.facebook.com/progressiveloveacademy

The website for the Progressive Love™ Academy is:
http://progressiveloveacademy.com

PROGRESSIVE LOVE ACADEMY

The Progressive Love™ Academy is your #1 relationship tools and information resource school on the web for creating your life and ideal relationship. No other online relationship school has the number of tools, resources, and certification courses.

With resources, courses, and certifications like:

- UPLVL Communication™ Certification
- The Relationship Tools Video Library
- The Trust Forum
- The Three-Way Mirror Certification Course
- Feminine Power 101
- The Blue Butterfly Women's Empowerment
- The Peaceful Warrior Men's Development

For more information, go to:
http://www.progressiveloveacademy.com

UPLVL Communication™
The Ultimate Solution to Save Relationships and Eliminate Hurtful, Damaging, & Meaningless Arguments

Learn the world's greatest communication protocol to eliminate arguments and misunderstandings in relationships. Find out how to be heard by your partner while learning the skills also to listen to them. This system has saved thousands of relationships and marriages.

Available on Amazon

Change Your Man: How to Become the Woman He Wants

Learn the secrets of femininity and how to find true love in your life. Attract the man of your dreams by learning to change the inner you. Don't allow your inner man to stop you from attracting the man you've always desired. In this book, Kenya K. Stevens discusses the secrets she used to attract her husband and find true love.

Available on Amazon

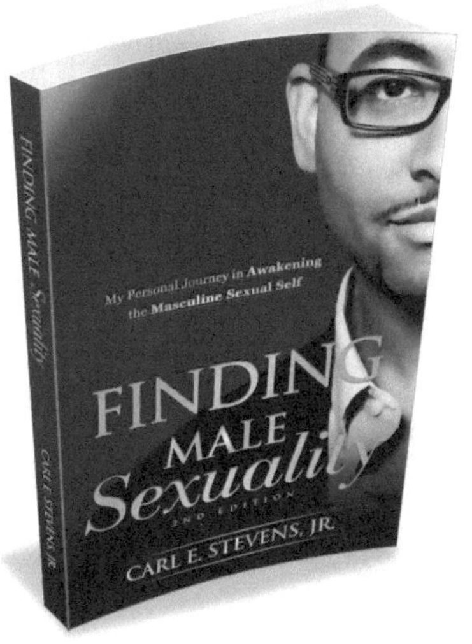

Finding Male Sexuality: My Personal Journey in Awakening the Masculine Sexual Self

Continue your learning experience by reading the second edition of Finding Male Sexuality: My Personal Journey in Awakening the Masculine Sexual Self. This book illustrates many of my sexual experiences that were critical in awakening my sexual power and skill as an effective lover to my many partners. Part 2 of the book gives practical exercises any man can use to awaken his sexual mastery.

Available on Amazon

The Art of Open Relating: Volume 1 – Theory, Philosophy, & Foundation

Continue your learning experience by reading The Art of Open Relating: Volume 1 – Theory, Philosophy, & Foundation to expand your knowledge of open relating and alternative styles of love. Examine the additional relationship styles available and determine if a freedom-based relating model is right for you.

Available on Amazon

The Art of Open Relating: Volume 3 – Trials, Tribulations, & Lessons Learned

Continue your learning experience by reading The Art of Open Relating: Volume 3 – Trials, Tribulations, & Lessons Learned by getting sneak peak into Carl's open relationship life. See how Carl and Kenya went from a monogamous marriage to an open marriage. Read about Carl's many relationships as an open relator and the ups and downs he experienced throughout.

Available on Amazon

Made in United States
Troutdale, OR
11/20/2023

14763445R00120